U. S. DEPARTMENT

DIVISION OF

BULLETI

GRASSES OF THE SOUTHWEST.

PLATES AND DESCRIPTIONS

OF THE

GRASSES OF THE DESERT REGION OF WESTERN TEXAS, NEW MEXICO,
ARIZONA, AND SOUTHERN CALIFORNIA.

Part I.

By Dr. GEO. VASEY,

BOTANIST. DEPARTMENT OF AGRICULTURE.

PUBLISHED BY AUTHORITY OF THE SECRETARY OF AGRICULTURE.

WASHINGTON:
GOVERNMENT PRINTING OFFICE
1890.

NOTE.

This Bulletin is to constitute the first half of the first volume of a work entitled "Illustrations of North American Grasses." The work when completed will consist of two volumes, the first entitled "Grasses of the Southwest," the second, "Grasses of the Pacific Slope." Proper title-pages and indexes will be published with the last part of each volume.

LETTER OF TRANSMITTAL.

WASHINGTON, *June 5,* 1890.

SIR: I have the honor of presenting for publication the manuscript of a Bulletin the Grasses of the Southwest.

Respectfully,

GEORGE VASEY,
Botanist.

Hon. J. M. RUSK,
Secretary of Agriculture.

INTRODUCTION.

The region of country immediately adjoining the northern boundary of Mexico, including the western part of Texas, and the greater part of New Mexico, Arizona, and southern California, is one of remarkable heat and aridity. It is mainly a region of elevated plains, called mesas, intersected by mountain ranges which occasionally run into high peaks, and is drained by comparatively few streams, which, on account of the limited rain-fall, cease to flow during a good part of the year, or convey only the waters obtained from distant portions of the country.

Most of the region lies north of the thirty-second parallel of latitude, and in the western part reaches into Utah and Nevada. It is with great propriety called the desert belt. The country northward, and east of the Rocky Mountains, as far as the one hundredth meridian, is an elevated arid plain, but with more abundant grasses, although rarely forming a continuous and connected sod.

In the desert belt, however, the grasses become scanty, not in variety of species, but in distribution, some of them being short-lived, springing up suddenly after the summer rains and rapidly maturing; others perennial, growing in bunches, and having deeply penetrating roots which enable them to endure the long droughts of the country. Nowhere do the native grasses form a continuous sod, but grow in scattered bunches in connection with the low bushes which prevail on the mesas or among the chaparral.

The country embraced in this desert belt is an extension northward of the great plateau of northern Mexico, as is shown in the similar character of its vegetation. The grasses are largely the same, or of the same genera. But the grasses, like the rest of the vegetation, are peculiar to the region. Here one never sees the common grasses of the Eastern States. The vegetation is as different from that of the Eastern States as is that of the northern portion of the Sahara. Hence arises the utility of bringing to the notice of the public, and especially of the residents of this region, the information contained in this work. It is not a manual or description of all the grasses of the region, but it furnishes illustrations and descriptions of some of the more interesting and some of the commoner grasses of the country. Many of them were observed and specimens collected by the naturalists of the Mexican Boundary Survey, and by those of the Pacific Railroad Survey, but few or none of these have heretofore been illustrated or fully described. True, the descriptions here given are mostly in technical language, but accompanied by the illustrations they afford the best possible means of recognition. Probably the most important agricultural question before the people of this region is how to increase the production of grasses and forage plants on the arid lands. It is the opinion of many that this can be done by bringing under cultivation some of the native species. Experiments are about to be undertaken in this direction by the Agricultural Experiment Stations and by individuals. The first step in such an enterprise is a knowledge of or an acquaintance with the native species. Nothing can be better adapted to this object than the work here undertaken, and in this way the knowledge of the scientist can be made helpful to the practical economist. In this first part of the work fifty plates of grasses are given. A second part of an equal number of plates is now in preparation, after which it is proposed to publish an analytical synopsis of all the grasses of the desert region. The drawings of the grasses have been made chiefly by Mr. William R. Scholl, and in the description of the species I wish to acknowledge important aid from Mr. Frederick V. Coville, Assistant Botanist.

INDEX OF PLATES.

GRASSES OF THE SOUTHWEST.

PART I.

ERIOCHLOA SERICEA Munro.

Roots long, unbranched, but giving off a few fibrillæ.

Culms tufted, simple, ½ to 3 feet high, stiffly erect, slender, striate, short-villous at the nodes and sparingly minutely hairy where not sheathed.

Radical *leaves* numerous, 6 to 12 inches long, erect, flat or involute, striate, minutely pubescent or glabrous, ½ to 1 line broad, the sheaths free. Cauline leaves 3 or 4; sheaths contiguous or nearly so, striate, minutely pubescent or glabrous, villous at the apex; ligule a row of dense straight hairs; blades like those of the root-leaves, spreading, 3 to 9 inches long, uppermost often shorter.

Inflorescence a racemose compound spike, the peduncle usually exserted from the uppermost sheath; axis minutely pubescent; spikes 4 to 7, sessile or the lower short-peduncled, erect, contiguous, or nearly so, ¾ to 1½ inches long.

Spikelets elliptical-oblong, acute, depressed, 1½ to 2 lines long, imbricated (one-half their length) in 2 rows along the outer side of the flat rachis of the spike, each sessile on an annular swelling of the apex of a short, long-villous pedicel (about as broad as long), hairs equaling the spikelet.

Glumes 3; outer 2 equal, membranaceous, inclosing the rest of the spikelet, ovate, oblong, acute, 5-nerved, villous without; flowering glume glabrous, thickened-coriaceous, minutely rugose, elliptical-oblong and acute, rounded on the back.

Flower single, hermaphrodite. Palet similar in texture to the flowering glume, 2-nerved, flat on the back. Stamens 3, the anthers two-thirds as long as the palet. Stigmas 2, fimbriate, purple, nearly one-half the length of the palet, on slender styles.

PLATE I; *a*, spikelet opened so as to show the glumes, palet, pistil, and stamens. In the figure the flowering glume is too much narrowed toward the apex, the palet is not represented as flat on the back, and the stigmas and anthers are too short.

This species seems to be principally confined to western Texas and New Mexico, extending northward into the Indian Territory. It affords a considerable quantity of foliage, is perennial, and should be tried with reference to its agricultural value.

a

PANICUM BULBOSUM H. B. K.

Rootstock creeping, slightly branching, the yearly growth short (commonly ¼ inch), base of the culm becoming enlarged into a corm ⅜ to ¾ inch long, or sometimes nearly wanting. Roots simple, strong.

Culms erect, single or few together in a loose clump, slender or stout (sometimes ¼ inch thick), simple, glabrous, glaucous at the nodes.

Leaves with striate blades 1 to 4 lines broad. Radical few, commonly 1 to 2 feet long; sheath elongated, loose, glabrous or the margins sometimes ciliate; blade glabrous or very sparingly hirsute at the base, slender-acuminate at the apex; ligule short, fimbriate. Sheaths of the stem 2 to 4, not contiguous, sheathing, glabrous; blades as in the radical leaves.

Inflorescence an exsert-pedunculate, usually open panicle 9 to 20 inches long; main axis glabrous or occasionally scabrous, pubescent at the forks; spikelets borne singly on short, scabrous pedicels, or sometimes sessile.

Spikelets 1½ to 2 lines long, nearly terete, elliptical-lanceolate to oblong, bluntly acute.

Glumes 4, glabrous, membranaceous, purple or pale green; 2 lower empty; first broadly ovate, acute, 3- to 7-nerved, frequently unsymmetrically, one-third to one-half the length of the spikelet; second as long as the spikelet, oblong, bluntly acute, 5- to 7-nerved.

Flowers 2. Lower staminate; glume like the second empty glume; palet hyaline, thin-membranaceous, 2-nerved. Upper flower hermaphrodite; glume coriaceous, minutely corrugated, obsoletely few-nerved, acute; palet 2-nerved, similar in texture to the glume; stamens 3; styles long.

PLATE II; *a*, three spikelets enlarged; *b*, spikelet opened to show the parts; *c*, portion of the base of the culm, and the corm of the preceding year. On the left, in *b*, in order from below, are the lower empty glume, first flowering glume, and palet of the staminate flower, on the right the second empty glume, the second flowering glume, and to the left of the stamens and pistil the palet of the fertile flower.

This grass should be one of great agricultural value. Its bulbous rootstocks contain a store of moisture which enables it to endure a protracted drought, and as it grows of large size it would produce a great amount of fodder.

PANICUM DIFFUSUM, H. B. K.

PANICUM CILIATISSIMUM Buckley.

Rootstock and roots slender.

Culms varying from erect at the ends of the rootstock to procumbent and even creeping, glabrous, except a ring of reflexed hairs at the nodes; erect stems from a few inches to 2 feet high, commonly with short sterile branches, slender, the internodes sometimes 3 inches long; creeping stems long, thicker, profusely branching, with shorter internodes, rooting at the nodes.

Leaves with long-ciliate, usually sparingly hirsute sheaths, and flat, smooth, or sometimes slightly hirsute blades tapering from base to apex. Sheaths of the erect stems frequently distant, those of the creeping stems shorter but mostly contiguous. Blades of the creeping stems seldom exceeding 1½ inches, those of the erect plants usually longer.

Inflorescence a small narrow panicle 2½ inches long or reduced to a few spikelets, terminating the culm, exsert-stipitate in the erect plant (in creeping plants terminating short axillary branches as well, and partly sheathed, all intermediate stages being found), bearing the spikelets terminal or laterally sessile on the flat minutely pubescent branches of the panicle.

Spikelets 1½ to 2 lines long, oblong, acuminate, slightly obcompressed.

Glumes 4; 3 lower membranaceous; first lanceolate, acuminate, glabrous, 3- to 5-nerved, nearly as long as the spikelet; second ovate, short-acuminate, pubescent, sometimes minutely villous-ciliate near the margins, many (about 11-)-nerved; third similar to the last, but glabrous down the middle, most of the nerves of that area obsolete; fourth (flowering) glume coriaceous, indistinctly few-nerved, minutely corrugated, bluntly acute.

Flowers 2. Lower reduced to a hyaline, 2-nerved, oblong palet subtended by the third glume; or sometimes with 3 stamens. Upper hermaphrodite; palet of the same texture as its glume, indistinctly 2-nerved; glume closely embracing the grain; stamens 3.

PLATE III; 1, erect stem; 2, creeping stem; *a* spikelet opened to show the parts.

PANICUM CILIATISSIMUM, *Buckley*

, PANICUM LACHNANTHUM Torrey.

Roots slender.

Culms closely tufted, with numerous short sterile branches from near the base, erect or ascending, 1 to 2½ feet high, slender, glabrous.

Leaves with flat blades 1 to 2 lines wide; sheaths from smooth to divaricately villous, those of the lower part of the stem long and far exceeding the short internodes, those (sheaths) of the rootstock densely soft villous; ligule about 1½ lines long, broadly obtuse, apical margin fimbriate; blade from glabrous to minutely pubescent, commonly 2 to 4 inches long.

Inflorescence a panicle on a long slender peduncle. Panicle contracted, 4 to 9 inches long, composed of 7 to 9 erect or appressed sessile branches 1 inch or more long; spikelets closely racemose on the branches; pedicel flat; branches of the panicle triangular, both with green scabrous angles.

Spikelets narrowly to broadly lanceolate-acuminate, 1½ to 2 lines long, showing an inclination toward an arrangement in 2 rows along the raceme.

Glumes 4; 3 lower membranaceous, empty; first a minute, hyaline, obtuse scale from ⅓ line long to nearly obsolete; second narrowly lanceolate, acuminate, 3- to 5-nerved, densely long-villous on the back, hairs when the grain is mature, spreading in all directions as if from a point in the center of the spikelet; third similar to the last but broader and about 5-nerved, its middle portion glabrous, intramarginal hairs as in the second glume and similarly spreading; fourth (flowering) glabrous, thin, coriaceous, with thin membranaceous margins, indistinctly 3-nerved, minutely roughened in longitudinal lines, lanceolate, acuminate, when mature chestnut-brown.

Flower single, hermaphrodite. Palet similar in texture, shape, and color to the flowering glume, nerveless. Stamens 3; anthers ¼ line long, one-half as broad. Stigmas long, cylindrical.

Grain inclosed by the palet and its glume, oval, obcompressed, white, slightly exceeding ⅔ line long.

PLATE IV; *a*, spikelet opened to show its parts, on the left the second glume and flowering glume, on the right the third glume and palet. The first glume, which should stand on the right, is omitted; the inflexed membranaceous margins of the flowering glume and palet are not shown; and the ovary is represented as of the size of a mature grain with the anthers twice their real length.

This grass grows freely on stony hills, and probably is capable of resisting drought. It seems deserving of trial as an agricultural grass for the southwest.

PANICUM LACHNANTHUM, *Torr.*

SETARIA CAUDATA R. & S.

Plant annual.

Rootstock none. Roots slender.

Culms 2 to 2½ foot high, branching from the base, scabrous or nearly glabrous; nodes provided with a ring of silky appressed hairs; branches usually short and sterile.

Leaves of the stem 4 or 5; sheaths usually distant, glabrous, ciliate on the margins, villous at the apex; blade 1 to 3 lines broad, usually 5 to 9 inches long, flat, glabrous beneath, scabrous above; ligule about 1 line long, cut nearly to the base into silky hairs. Radical leaves like those of the stem.

Inflorescence a contracted spike-like panicle 3 to 4 lines broad (exclusive of the bristles), 3 to 6 inches long, on a moderately long exserted peduncle; branches of the panicle short (1 to 3 lines), spikelets sessile or nearly so, some of the pedicels sterile and prolonged into slender scabrous bristles 6 lines long or less. Spikelets ovate, acute, semi-terete, 1 to 1½ lines long.

Glumes 4; 2 lower empty, membranaceous, glabrous; first broadly ovate, acute, 3-nerved, one-half the length of spikelet; second broadly oval, obtuse or mucronate, 5-nerved, nearly as long as the spikelet, fitting closely to the flowering glume; third like the second but slightly longer, acute, and subtending a rudimentary lanceolate hyaline palet; fourth (flowering), when in position, narrowly ovate, acute, coriaceous, rounded and minutely rugose-roughened on the back, obscurely 5-nerved.

Flower hermaphrodite. Palet lanceolate when in position, coriaceous (the infolded margins membranaceous), flat on the back when mature, obscurely 2-nerved. Stamens 3. Stigmas 2, oblong.

PLATE V; *a*, spikelet with its accompanying bristle. The spikelet is opened to show its parts. The flowering glume is represented too short, and should be acute, while the back of the palet is not represented as flat.

This grass has much the habit of German millet, and with proper cultivation would probably produce an abundant crop.

SETARIA CAUDATA, *R. & S.*

CENCHRUS MYOSUROIDES H. B. K.

Culms erect or from an ascending base, usually simple, 2 to 4 feet high, stout, glabrous, glaucous.

Leaves of the stem 6 to 10; sheaths glabrous, nearly contiguous; blade glabrous to minutely strigose, flat or sometimes involute, 2 to 4 lines wide, commonly 5 to 12 inches long; ligule fimbriate to the base. Radical leaves early dying.

Inflorescence a short-pedunculate or partly sheathed, compact, erect spike 3 to 4 lines thick, 3 to 8 inches long, rachis minutely pubescent, spikelets borne singly.

Spikelets 2 to 2½ lines long surrounded at the base by a ring of many retrosely barbed stiff bristles of different lengths, the longest equaling the spikelets; body lanceolate, acute, terete.

Glumes 4: first membranaceous, ovate, 1- to 3-nerved, acute, one-half the length of the spikelet; second membranaceous, ovate, 5- to 7-nerved, acute, equaling the spikelet; third like the second, but subtending a hyaline 2-nerved palet (this lanceolate when in position); fourth (flowering) like the second and third, but rather coriaceous, the nerves more obscure and seldom green.

Flower hermaphrodite. Palet similar in shape and texture to its glume, but 2-nerved. Stamens 3, anthers linear, about 1 line long. Stigmas 2, linear.

Grain ¾ line long, somewhat obcompressed, quadrangular, oblong. very obtuse, with an embryo three-fourths as long, when mature inclosed in the glumes and bristles, the whole falling off together.

PLATE VI; *a*, spikelet closed; *b*, spikelet opened, the bristles removed. On the right in *b* are the first glume, third glume and sterile palet, on the left the second glume, flowering glume, and its palet.

This grass will grow in very dry soil, and will produce a good crop of forage, but is somewhat objectionable on account of the prickly seed-envelopes.

CENCHRUS MYOSUROIDES, *H. B. K.*

CENCHRUS TRIBULOIDES L.

Plant annual. Roots slender.

Culms glabrous, a few inches to 3 feet high, usually branching from the base and procumbent, rooting at the lower nodes, or sometimes the shorter plants erect.

Leaves of the stem 3 to 10; sheaths glabrous, rarely ciliate on the margins above, usually loose, commonly contiguous; blade 6 inches long or less, 1 to 2 lines broad, flat or sometimes involute; ligule about ½ line long, deeply densely fimbriate.

Inflorescence a short-pedunculate or partly sheathed spike of clusters, 4 inches long or reduced to a single cluster, the rachis nearly smooth. Clusters composed of 2 to 3 spikelets surrounded by an involucre. Involucre thick, coriaceous, cleft to the base on the side next the rachis or on both sides, inclosing the spikelets; the outer surface provided with numerous bristles and spines flattened below and retrorsely barbed, those toward the base of the involucre smaller, the larger 2½ lines long.

Spikelets 2 to 3 in each involucre, 1 at least fully developed and with the following structure (the others rudimentary in various degrees).

Glumes 4; 3 lower membranaceous; first short, ovate, acute, 1- to 3-nerved, empty; second broadly lanceolate, 5-nerved, acute, nearly as long as the involucre, empty; third like the second, but subtending a flower; fourth (flowering) a little larger and similar in form to the second and third, but thin-coriaceous.

Flowers 2. Lower staminate, with a thin hyaline 2-nerved palet; stamens 3. Upper with a thin-coriaceous palet, hermaphrodite; ovary flattened, circular in outline; stamens 3, anthers ½ line long, dehiscing much earlier than those of the staminate flower.

Grain inclosed in the spikelet, spikelet inclosed in the involucre, the whole disarticulating from the spike together.

PLATE VII; *a*, external view of the involucre; *b*, the same cut open to show the spikelets; *c*, a single fully developed spikelet opened to show the parts. On the left are the second glume, the fourth glume, and the hermaphrodite flower; on the right are the first glume, the third glume, and the staminate flower. The first glume should be inserted below the second, and is represented twice too long, as are the anthers of the hermaphrodite flower.

This species is too common in sandy grounds, where its spiny burs are an annoyance to men and beasts and an injury to the wool of sheep that graze near it.

CENCHRUS TRIBULOIDES, *Linn.*

STENOTAPHRUM AMERICANUM Schrank.

Rootstock apparently creeping.   Roots fibrous-branched.

Culms creeping and rooting at the nodes, or procumbent, from 2 feet long to very short, simple or with a few main branches, glabrous, enlarged at the nodes, and there provided with a short sterile branch or fascicle of leaves.

Leaves of the stem several, pale green; sheaths glabrous, or slightly ciliate on the margin above, usually loose and not contiguous; blade 2 to 3 lines wide, from 8 inches long to very short, flat, thick (nerves obscure, midrib prominent beneath), glabrous, abruptly rounded at the apex, rarely acute; ligule minute, densely fimbriate.

Inflorescence a usually sheathed spike terminating the stem and main branches; rachis thickened and enlarged (reaching 3 lines in diameter and 4 inches in length); spikelets embedded singly sessile, or with 1 to 3 additional short-pedicellate ones, at each joint, arranged along 2 nearly opposite sides of the rachis but facing one way.

Spikelets lanceolate-ovate, 1½ to 2½ lines long.

Glumes 4; first membranaceous, hyaline, small, nerveless, and obtuse or sometimes one-half the length of the spikelet; second membranaceous, 7- to 11-nerved, ovate, acute, as long as the spikelet, empty; third similar in form, somewhat coriaceous, but 5-nerved, subtending a flower; fourth like the third, but more coriaceous, also subtending a flower.

Flowers 2. Lower staminate; stamens 3; palet coriaceous below, 2-nerved. Upper flower hermaphrodite; stamens 3; stigmas 2, cylindrical or club-shaped.

PLATE VIII; figure below at the right, joint of the rachis showing 2 spikelets, the lower sessile, the upper pedicelled; at the left, spikelet opened to show the parts. In the flower on the right, which is the hermaphrodite one, the stigmas should be twice as long and proportionally broader. The stamens have matured earlier and are not shown.

This grass grows in sandy land especially near the sea-coast. It has strong creeping roots, which render it capable of enduring great drought. It has been recommended in Florida as a very valuable pasture grass.

STENOTAPHRUM AMERICANUM, *Schkr.*

THURBERIA ARKANSANA Bentham.

Plant annual.

Rootstock none. Roots very slender.

Culms erect, simple or branching from the base, slender, commonly 9 to 18 inches high, sometimes depauperate, glabrous.

Leaves of the stem 3 to 5; sheaths contiguous, glabrous or sparingly villous, the margin villous-ciliate; blade flat, 1 to 4 inches long, 1 to 2 lines broad, flaccid, scabrous, and usually sparingly minutely villous-pubescent; ligule about $\frac{1}{2}$ line long, the apex narrowly fringed.

Inflorescence a panicle at first partly sheathed, finally pedunculate, 3 to 6 inches long; branches slender, seldom exceeding 1 inch in length; spikelets borne singly on pedicels $1\frac{1}{2}$ lines long or shorter.

Spikelets linear, $1\frac{1}{2}$ to 2 lines long (exclusive of the awn), nearly terete, jointed to the pedicel below the glumes.

Glumes 3; first and second of equal length, similar, lanceolate, acute, green, nerveless or obsoletely 3-nerved, scabrous-pubescent without, apices slightly separated; third (flowering) not green except the 3 nerves, glabrous, rather thick, lanceolate, folded and compressed, awned on the back a little below the apex; apex cleft half-way to the origin of the awn; awn slender, $\frac{1}{4}$ to $\frac{1}{2}$ inch long, little twisted, abruptly bent at the middle.

Flower single, hermaphrodite; rachilla prolonged above the flower (!) into a minute filiform rudiment about $\frac{1}{2}$ line long, naked or surmounted by a minute scale; palet very thin, hyaline, narrowly linear, 2-nerved; lodicules 2, about $\frac{1}{2}$ line long; stamens 3, anther oblong, about $\frac{1}{4}$ line long; stigmas cylindrical, on short distant styles.

Grain linear-oblong, remaining closed within the glumes, the spikelet disarticulating below them.

Plate IX; *a*, first (on the left) and second glumes; *b*, flowering glume and flower. The rudimentary prolongation of the rachilla shown in *b* is usually twice as long and is inserted at a point on the axis near the middle of the base of the palet, not on the flowering glume, as shown in the figure.

THURBERIA ARKANSANA, *Benth.*

HILARIA CENCHROIDES H. B. K., var. TEXANA Vasey.

Plant perennial.

Rootstock none. Roots slender, branching.

Stems of two kinds, (1) runners and (2) normal culms. Runners with 1 or few nodes, producing a plant at each; internodes several inches long, slender, terete, glabrous. Culms erect, 6 to 12 inches high, slender, densely tufted from a single rootstock, glabrous, retrosely long-villous at the nodes.

Leaves of the stem 2 to 4; sheaths about 1 inch long, distant, tightly sheathing, glabrous; blade ½ to 1 line wide, seldom exceeding 3 inches in length, flat, scabrous above and on the margins, rarely beneath, otherwise smooth except sometimes a few long hairs. Root-leaves similar, several on each stem, sheaths imbricated.

Inflorescence a usually slender-pedunculate spike ¾ to 1¼ inches long; rachis flat, zigzag, minutely pubescent, spikelets inserted in clusters of 3 (resembling a single spikelet) on opposite sides, contiguous or one-half overlapping.

Spikelets 2¼ to 3½ lines long, the parts spreading above.

(1) MIDDLE SPIKELETS.

Glumes 3; first and second equal, similar, nearly as long as the spikelet, body many-nerved, coriaceous below, scabrous, compressed, at the middle separating into two linear obtuse spreading lobes becoming membranaceous-hyaline at the apex, bearing in the fork an awn slightly exceeding the spikelet; third (flowering) broadly oblong below, hyaline, 3-nerved, compressed, abruptly tapering from below the middle into a slender compressed neck.

Flower pistillate. Palet similar to the flowering glume but narrower and 2-nerved, and with it forming a cavity below and a neck above. Ovary and afterward the grain inclosed in this cavity. Styles long, lying in the neck, very slender above; stigmas cylindrical, the body thick.

(2) LATERAL SPIKELETS.

Glumes 4; first similar to that of the middle spikelet, but inequilateral, and with shorter awn; second similar to the first but merely mucronate; third and fourth each subtending a flower, alike, thin-membranaceous, lanceolate, hyaline, 1-nerved or with 1 or 2 additional lateral nerves.

Flowers staminate. Palet thin-membranaceous, hyaline, 2-nerved, linear. Stamens 3, anther narrowly linear.

Grain inclosed primarily in its palet and glume, these becoming shining-coriaceous, the whole inclosed in the empty glumes, the entire cluster of spikelets dropping off together.

PLATE X; *a*, cluster of three spikelets; *b*, staminate flowers of one of the lateral spikelets; *c*, pistillate flower of the middle spikelet. In *b*, one of the spikelets should be sessile. In *c*, the stigmas are nearly twice too short and proportionally too narrow, their bodies too slender, and the filaments not thick enough below.

This species differs from the Mexican type in being more slender, with longer culms, more spikelets in the spike, and the spikelets narrower and smooth instead of scabrous.

HILARIA CENCHROIDES, *H. B. K.*

HILARIA MUTICA Bentham. .

Plants perennial.

Roots thick, simple, with a cork-like covering.   Rootstock creeping, woody, scaly-sheathed.

Culms erect or from an ascending base, 9 to 20 inches high, somewhat tufted, usually with many sterile branches below, glabrous, sometimes hairy at the nodes.

Leaves of the stem 4 to 10; sheaths imbricated below, distant above, glabrous, the margins sometimes ciliate above; blade 1 to 1½ lines broad, reaching 6 inches long, flat or involute, usually slightly scabrous, otherwise smooth; ligule about ½ line long, fimbriate.

Inflorescence a close spike, pedunculate or scarcely exserted, 1¼ to 3 inches long; spikelets arranged in clusters of 3 on opposite sides of. the flat rachis, imbricated.

Spikelets 2 to 3 lines long, with a tuft of long hairs surrounding the cluster at the base.

(1) MIDDLE SPIKELETS.

Glumes 3; first and second alike, oblanceolate, 1-nerved at the base, with ciliate membranaceous margins, the nerve splitting above into several branches, continued into short aristæ, or the lateral ones joined into a fimbriate membrane; third (flowering) glume membranaceous, linear, obtuse, 3-nerved.

Flower hermaphrodite.   Stamens 3; anther narrow-linear, ½ to 2 lines long, the narrow cells free at the ends.   Styles 2, long; stigmas long, narrow-cylindrical, with thick bodies, exserted from the apex of the tube formed by the palet and glume.

(2) LATERAL SPIKELETS.

Glumes commonly 5 to 6; two lower empty, upper successively shorter, apices of all even; first lanceolate, several-nerved, ciliate on the membranaceous margins and apex, usually with a short lateral awn on the margin nearest the middle spikelet; second similar, but linear and unawned; flowering glumes narrowly quadrangular-oblong, truncate, membranaceous, 3-nerved.

Flowers staminate.   Palet similar to the glume but narrower, 2-nerved. Stamens 3, similar to those of the middle spikelet, those of the upper flowers successively shorter.

Grain inclosed in the finally coriaceous and shining flowering glume and palet, these remaining attached in the cluster of spikelets, the whole dropping off together.

PLATE XI; *a*, two lateral spikelets of a cluster, and *b*, middle spikelet opened to show the parts.   The cluster is viewed from the side toward the rachis of the spike.   The lateral awn of the two glumes uppermost in *a* is not shown, nor are the stamens of the upper flowers of the lateral spikelets shown.   In *b*, the styles are those of an unopened flower, and in all cases the cells of the anthers are represented as united even to their ends.

This species and another similar one (*H. Jamesii*) are called *gietta* by the Mexicans, and in some localities also called 'black grama.'   In southern New Mexico and Arizona they are the prevailing grama grasses, taking the place of the white grama (*Bouteloua oligostachya*) which covers the plains of western Kansas and Nebraska.   The species here described is one of the most important forage grasses of this region.

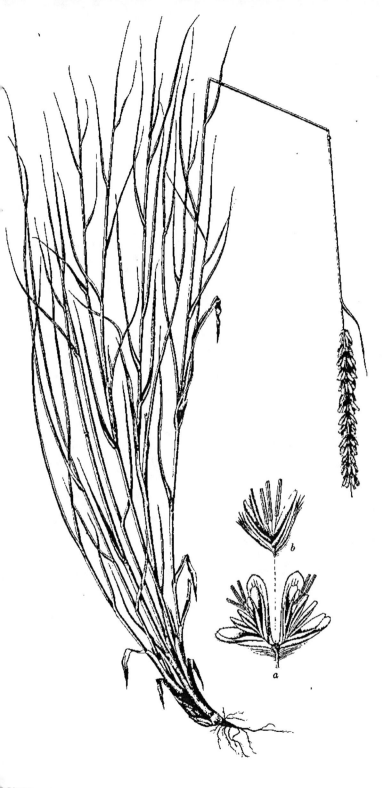

HILARIA MUTICA, *Benth.*

ÆGOPOGON GEMINIFLORUS H.'B. K.*

Plant annual.

Culms procumbent and branching at the base, or even creeping and rooting at the lower nodes; erect parts about 1 foot high, very slender, glabrous.

Leaves of the stem 3 to 6; sheaths slender, glabrous, usually not quite contiguous; blade ½ to 1 line broad, ¼ inch long, flat, flaccid, glabrous; ligule conspicuous, about 1 line long, the apex short-lacerate.

Inflorescence racemose; spikelets in umbels of 3, one nearly sessile; umbels on short, slender, scabrous peduncles, usually turned to one side, in a raceme 1¼ to 3 inches long; rachis slender, scabrous.

Spikelets lanceolate, acute, excluding the awns about 2 lines long, pedicelled ones a little smaller.

Glumes 3; first and second similar, 1-nerved, made up of a narrow body excurrent into an awn, and 2 narrow, lateral, membranaceous, from truncate to acuminate wings (one shorter than the other); third (flowering) lanceolate, 3-nerved, each nerve excurrent into an awn, middle one (shorter in the pedicelled spikelets) nearly as long as the spikelet, lateral ones minute.

Flower single, hermaphrodite. Palet membranaceous, lanceolate, 2-nerved, each nerve excurrent into a minute tooth. Stamens 3, anthers about ¾ line long, linear, the cells joined only at the middle. Stigmas short, cylindrical.

Grain not seen, but probably inclosed in the spikelets, the umbel of 3 dropping off together.

PLATE XII; lower figure, cluster of three spikelets; upper figure, spikelet opened to show the parts. The lateral lobes of the first and second glumes are broader and usually less acute than in the figure. In the upper figure the position of the first glumes is reversed, and in both figures the stamens and pistils are omitted.

---

* This description was made from a single set of specimens cultivated from Mexican seed. They are taken to be the typical form of H. B. K. Several forms whose specific relationships have not all been well worked out occur in the southwestern United States and Mexico, and none of them, although they may prove to be varieties of this species, were noted in writing the description.

ÆGOPOGON GEMINIFLORUS, *H. B. K.*

CATHESTECUM ERECTUM Vasey & Hackel.

Plant peronnial.

Roots slender. Rootstock none.

Stems of two kinds, (1) runners and (2) erect culms. Runners slender, with internodes few to several inches long, glabrous, arcuate, giving rise to a new plant at each node. Culms densely tufted below, many of them short and leafy, a few elongated, very slender, 6 to 10 inches high, glabrous.

Leaves of the root numerous; sheath short, ¼ to 1 inch long, glabrous, long-ciliate at the apex; blade 3 inches or less long, about ¼ line wide, scabrous on the margins, otherwise glabrous or rarely with a few long hairs; ligule minute, fimbriate. Leaves of the stems 2 or 3; sheaths about 1 inch long, distant, otherwise like those of the root; blade from 1 inch long to almost wanting.

Inflorescence racemose; spikelets in a raceme of 4 to 8 clusters; racemes slender-pedunculate, about 1 inch long, single or 2 or 3 together from the uppermost sheath; rachis very slender, flat, glabrous or slightly scabrous; clusters short-pedicellate, composed of 3 spikelets, middle spikelet short-pedicelled, lateral nearly sessile.

Glumes 4 to 6; first small, truncate-cuneate, empty, nearly nerveless; second empty, lanceolate, 1-nerved; others subtending flowers, 4-lobed, 3-nerved, more or less scabrous on the back, the nerves extending into a short scabrous awn between the lobes.

Flowers 3 to 4, hermaphrodite (?); palet lanceolate, 2-nerved, stamens 3, anthers 1 to 1½ lines long; pistils not detected; sterile prolongation of the rachilla sometimes found at the apex of the spikelets.

Grain not found.

PLATE XIII; *a*, cluster of spikelets; *b*, first glume; *c*, second glume; *d* and *e*, two flowering glumes; *f*, palet, from the back; *g* and *h*, palets, from the front; *i*, sterile prolongation of the rachilla; *j*, stamens and pistils; *k*, anther and upper portion of filament.

This grass is found on the arid bluffs of the Rio Grande in Texas, and westward near the Mexican border as far as Sonora. It is too small to be of much economic importance.

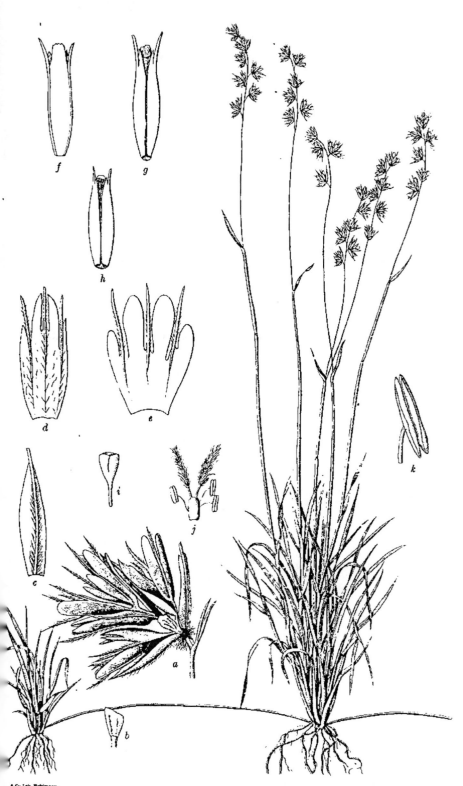

CATHESTECHUM ERECTUM, *Vasey et Hackel.*

TRAGUS RACEMOSUS Hall.

Plant annual.

Roots very slender.

Stem branching and procumbent at the base, sometimes rooting at the lower nodes, glabrous, 15 inches or less in height; depauperate plants sometimes simple, erect, and but 2 to 3 inches high.

Leaves of the stem 3 to 6; sheaths usually not contiguous, glabrous, often somewhat swollen; blade 1 to 2 lines broad, 1 to 2 inches long, or the uppermost nearly obsolete, glabrous except the coarsely ciliate-toothed margins, thick, pale green; ligule a dense row of short hairs.

Inflorescence a dense cylindrical spike of clusters of spikelets 2½ to 3½ lines thick, 1 to 4 inches long, frequently sheathed at the base, never long-peduncled; clusters nearly sessile, arranged singly on all sides of the terete minutely pubescent rachis.

Spikelets 2 to 3 in each cluster, closely spiked (backs together) on a short rachis; uppermost commonly reduced to a single echinate glume; lowest and usually the middle one perfect; rachis sometimes produced as a rudiment above the base of the upper flower.

Glumes 3; first ovate, small, thin, hyaline, nerveless; second thick, ovate to lanceolate, acute, the back ridged with several (commonly 5 to 7) nerves converging at the apex and beset with hooked spines; third (flowering) lanceolate, acute, mucronate-awned, slightly coriaceous, glabrous, 3-nerved.

Flower single, hermaphrodite. Palet lanceolate, membranaceous, 2-nerved. Stamens 3; anthers short, oblong; stigmas cylindrical, slender.

Grain light-brown, oblanceolate-oblong, slightly obcompressed, apiculate, short-stipitate, about ½ line long.

PLATE XIV; *a*, cluster of two spikelets opened to show the parts. The spikelet on the right shows the first glume (very small), the second glume (echinate), the flowering glume and its palet, and between them an organ probably meant to represent an anther. The spikelet to the left shows the same parts except the first glume which is replaced by the rudimentary prolongation of the rachis. The second spikelet should be raised on a slight prolongation of the rachis.

This is a widely distributed semi-tropical grass, not of economic value.

a

TRAGUS RACEMOSUS, *Hall.*

No. 15.

ELIONURUS BARBICULMIS Hackel.

Rootstock not seen, apparently creeping. Roots rather thick, mostly simple, unbranched, with a thin brown bark.

Culms densely tufted, erect, 1 to 3 feet high, slender, rigid, below the nodes pilose, a little lower scabrous, and lower yet glabrous; many short, producing only leaves.

Leaves of the stem 3 to 5; sheaths slender, usually not contiguous, glabrous, sparingly long-ciliate on the margins above; blade 8 inches long or less, the uppermost often entirely wanting, about ½ line wide, closely involute, long-pilose on the margins below, densely hairy for a short distance from the ligule within, otherwise glabrous, rising erect from the sheath; ligule a dense row of stiff hairs. Root leaves and those of the abortive stems similar to the last, but reaching 1 foot in length, tips frequently flexuous.

Inflorescence a more or less pedunculate terminal distichous spike, 2 to 4 inches long, about 3 lines thick, densely villous on both the rachis, pedicels, and spikelets; rachis flat.

Spikelets inserted 2 together on one side of the rachis at each joint; one sessile, 3 to 4 lines long; other pedicelled, of about the same length, including the pedicel.

Glumes 4; first lanceolate, several-nerved, densely villous on the back, apex bifid into two slender points; second lanceolate, 3-nerved, more or less villous in the middle of the back, these two inclosing the rest of the spikelet; third thin, membranaceous, laterally 2-nerved, ciliate on the inflexed margins; fourth (flowering) lanceolate, membranaceous, 1- to 3-nerved, glabrous.

Flower of sessile spikelet hermaphrodite; palet lanceolate, minute, membranaceous; lodicules 2, about ¼ line long, thick; stamens 3, linear, anthers 1½ to 2 lines long; stigmas long, cylindrical. Flower of pedicelled spikelet staminate; palet wanting, lodicules as in the hermaphrodite flower; stamens 3, shorter than the others.

Grain light-brown, obcompressed, elliptical-lanceolate, acute at each end; embryo occupying half its length. Rachis of the spike finally disarticulating just below the nodes, bearing the 2 spikelets, one containing the grain.

PLATE XV; *a*, portion of the rachis of the spike, showing the two spikelets at a node, opened to show their parts. The palet of the lower spikelets is not shown.

This species occurs on rocky hills in western Texas, southern New Mexico, and Arizona, and the adjacent parts of Mexico.

ELIONURUS BARBICULMUM, *Hack.*

No. 16.

HETEROPOGON CONTORTUS R. & S.

Rootstock short. Roots stout.

Culms tufted, smooth, branching above, erect, about 3 feet high.

Leaves 6 to 12 inches long, upper ones gradually shorter; blade flat, upper surface and margins rough, lower surface smooth; sheath smooth, much flattened.

Inflorescence spicate, cylindrical, about 2 inches long without the awns, main rachis smooth.

Spikelets 3 to 5 lines long, in pairs, lower sessile and perfect, upper on a short pedicel, and staminate only. Male spikelets turned to one side of the spike, almost concealing the fertile ones.

Glumes in the female spikelets 4, outer hard, hairy, convolute; second much narrower, hard, 3-nerved; third very thin, hyaline, smaller; fourth hyaline at the base, above extended into a hard twisted and bent awn 2 to 3 inches long or more. Glumes of the male spikelet 4; first ovate-lanceolate, flattish, keeled near the margin, thick, green, ciliate, many-nerved, margins thin; second thinner, narrower, 3-nerved, ciliate on the margin; third and fourth hyaline, somewhat shorter.

Stamens 3. Styles 2.

PLATE XVI; *a*, a pair of spikelets, the upper male, the lower female, with the long twisted and pubescent awn; *b*, a male flower spread open to show the parts. The fourth glume is omitted.

This grass furnishes a large amount of foliage, and is deserving of trial in cultivation.

HETEROPOGON CONTORTUS, R. & S.

TRACHYPOGON POLYMORPHUS Hack.

Rootstock short. Roots strong.

Culms tufted, smooth, bearded at the joints, unbranched, erect, 2 to 3 feet high.

Leaves. Lower ones 6 to 12 inches long, about 2 lines wide, attenuated to a point, scabrous, sparingly hairy toward the base; sheaths hairy, the lower ones longer than the internodes, the upper shorter; ligule 1 to 2 lines long, ovate-lanceolate, sparingly hairy.

Inflorescence a narrow, slender spike, rather loose, 4 to 6 inches long, erect; the rachis slightly hairy at the joints, otherwise smooth.

Spikelets in pairs, 3 to 4 lines long, each 1-flowered, the lower flower sessile and male only, the other on a short pedicel and perfect. Male spikelets: first and second glumes thick; first oblong-linear, 7- to 9-nerved, sparsely pubescent, obtuse, ciliate at apex; second lanceolate-oblong, 3-nerved, acute; third and fourth thin, hyaline. Female spikelet like the male except the flowering glume: this terminating in a hairy, twisted awn, about 2 inches long. Stamens 3. Styles 2, stigmas plumose.

PLATE XVII; *a,* pair of spikelets opened to show the parts.

TRACHYPOGON POLYMORPHUS. *Hack.*

ANDROPOGON CIRRHATUS Hackel.

Rootstock short. Roots strong.

Culms tufted, 2 to 3 feet high, slender, branching above, of 6 to 8 joints; lateral branches arising singly, slender, becoming long-exserted.

Leaves. Sheaths narrow, close, smooth, striate; ligule short, truncate, smooth; blade 3 to 6 inches long, 1 to 2 lines wide, attenuated to a long acute point, rigid, smooth, except the roughish margins.

Inflorescence terminal on the culm and its branches, in a spike-like raceme about 2 inches long consisting of 10 to 15 joints; rachis smooth.

Spikelets in pairs. Female spikelets sessile, about 3 lines long; first glume linear-lanceolate, thick, 2-toothed at apex, smooth except the scabrous keel and margins, 7- to 9-nerved; second glume slightly shorter than the first, acute, much thinner, 3-nerved above, smooth; third glume one-fourth shorter than the first, hyaline, linear-oblong, obtuse, 2-nerved, ciliate on the margins; fourth glume as long as the third, hyaline, bifid, attached below to an awn 6 to 8 lines long. Male spikelet rather shorter than the female, about equaling its pedicel; pedicel smooth except a tuft of cilia near the apex; glumes 4, much as in the female, but without the awn of the third glume.

PLATE XVIII; *a*, pair of spikelets; *b*, female spikelet opened to show the parts; *c*, male spikelet opened.

This is related to the broomsedge (*A. scoparius*), and is rather rare.

ANDROPOGON CIRRHATUS, *Hack.*

ANDROPOGON HIRTIFLORUS Kunth.

Culms 2 to 4 feet high, densely tufted on a short rootstock, erect, rather slender and wiry, with generally single branches from the upper joints; lower internodes compressed, furrowed on the inner face; branches becoming long-exserted and flower-bearing at the extremity, smooth.

Leaves crowded below, distant above; lower sheaths compressed, short, with scattering hairs or nearly smooth; ligule membranaceous, short, truncate; blade flat, 2 to 6 inches long, 1 to 2 lines wide, firm and erect, rather scabrous, acuminate.

Inflorescence terminating the culm and branches as a loose, narrow, few-flowered, spike-like raceme, consisting of 10 to 20 joints, 2 to 3 inches long; branches slender, long-exserted from the sheaths.

Spikelets in pairs at the joints of the flattened hairy rachis, lower perfect and fertile, upper sterile. Perfect spikelet 4 lines long; glumes 4, two of hard texture and two hyaline; first linear-lanceolate, roughened on the back, covered with long white hairs; second thinner, keeled, without hairs, minutely scabrous; third hyaline, a little shorter than the second, slightly ciliate, deeply bifid, attached below to its twisted and bent awn, which is 8 or 10 lines long; fourth hyaline, entire, inclosing the proper flower. Sterile spikelet: pedicel about 2 lines long, flattened, cilate; glumes generally 2; first lanceolate, acuminate, green, thick, hirsute; second hyaline, inclosed by the first.

PLATE XIX; *a*, pair of spikelets, the perfect one sessile, and the sterile one on a pedicel; *b*, perfect flower with the glumes spread out. The outer or first glume does not show the long hairs.

This species also is related to *A. scoparius*. It is found on rocky hills in western Texas, in the Santa Catalina and Huachuca Mountains of Arizona, and in Mexico.

a

b

ANDROPOGON SACCHAROIDES Swartz.

Rootstock short. Roots strong.

Culms tufted, smooth (nodes bearded or in some forms smooth), simple or branched, erect, 2 to 4 feet high, often with 5 or 6 joints.

Lower *leaves* 1 foot or more long; blade flat, narrow, acuminate, somewhat scabrous on both surfaces and on the margins; sheaths smooth, striate, shorter than the internodes, open; ligules broadly ovate, laciniate.

Inflorescence paniculate, oblong, about 4 inches long, composed of numerous (20 to 50) closely approximate and appressed sessile spike-like branches 1 inch or more long ; spikelets imbricated.

Spikelets in pairs at the joints of the branches, one sessile and perfect, the other on a short pedicel and either male or imperfect. Perfect spikelets 2 lines long with 2 outer hard glumes and 2 inner hyaline ones; first about 7-nerved, sparsely hairy, 2-toothed at the apex, second obscurely 3-nerved, third and fourth hyaline, latter terminating in a twisted awn sometimes 8 or 10 lines long. Male or sterile spikelet on a pedicel of about its own length, consisting of only 1 linear, pubescent, 5- to 7-nerved, glume; pedicel covered with long, fine, white hairs.

PLATE XX; *a*, perfect spikelet; *b*, both the sterile and perfect spikelets.

This species is common on rocky banks and borders of streams. It extends northward to southern Colorado and Kansas, and deserves trial as an agricultural grass for dry and sandy lands. There are several varieties.

ANDROPOGON SACCHAROIDES, *Sw.*

ANDROPOGON WRIGHTII Hackel.

Rootstock thick. Roots very strong.

Culms cæspitose, 2 to 3 feet high, unbranched, smooth, slightly hairy at the nodes.

Leaves. Sheaths smooth, striate, shorter than the internodes; ligules 1 line long, obtuse, smooth; blades 5 to 12 inches long, 2 to 3 lines wide, light green, smooth, the margins scabrous.

Panicle 2 to 3 inches long, consisting of 5 to 7 clustered or approximate spike-like branches 1½ to 2 inches long, shortly pedicellate, erect, and densely flowered; rachis flattened, hairy, ciliate.

Spikelets about 3 lines long, in pairs, one female, one male. Female spikelet sessile, lance-oblong, hairy at the base, sparsely hairy on the back below; first glume thick, 7-nerved above; second nearly equal to the first, 3-nerved; third and fourth hyaline, fourth with an awn ½ inch long. Male spikelet on a ciliate pedicel of half its length, about 3 lines long; first glume 9- to 11-nerved at the base, ciliate on the margins above; second more acute, 3-nerved, ciliate; third hyaline, nearly equaling the second; fourth very minute or wanting.

PLATE XXI; *a*, pair of spikelets; *b*, female spikelet spread open to show the parts; *c*, male spikelet opened.

This resembles the preceding species, but is smaller and with fewer spikes. It is rare, at least north of the boundary.

ANDROPOGON WRIGHTII. *Hack.*

ARISTIDA ARIZONICA Vasey.

Rootstocks unknown. Roots rather stout, simple above, with a thin bark. *Culms* erect, simple, closely tufted, 1 to 2½ feet high, glabrous.

Leaves all radical or originating near the base of the culm; sheaths imbricated, glabrous, sometimes 6 inches long; blades commonly 3 to 5, sometimes 10 inches long, glabrous, involute when dry; ligules a minute dense ring of hairs.

Inflorescence an exsert-pedunculate panicle 4 to 12 inches long; branches short, rarely exceeding 2 inches, nearly erect; spikelets singly sessile or short pedunculate. *Spikelets* (excluding the awns) ½ to ¾ inch long, awl-shaped, nearly terete.

Glumes 3; first linear, two-thirds the length of the spikelet, membranaceous, 1-nerved, aristate, acute with 2 minute accessory teeth, the midnerve and awn-point scabrous; second as long as the spikelet, narrower than the first, similar to it, the awn-point a little longer; third (flowering) glume coriaceous, as long as the second, closely involute, very slender, scabrous; apex twisted two or three times, then produced into 3. straight, terete, not twisted, scabrous awns diverging when dry, usually a little longer than the spikelet; middle one slightly the longest; rachilla slightly elongated between the second and third glumes, densely villous.

Flower single, hermaphrodite. Palet minute, nearly 1 line long. Lodicules 2, lanceolate, as long as the palet. Stamens 3, anthers linear nearly 1 line long. Stigmas 2, cylindrical.

Grain awl-shaped, about 4 lines long, closely enwrapped in the flowering glume; rachilla disarticulating obliquely just above the second glume.

PLATE XXII; *a*, spikelet, empty glumes spread open; *b*, the same empty glumes removed, flowering glume open to show the palet and stamens. The stigmas are not shown.

A common grass of the mesas and hills, which early in the season furnishes good grazing for animals.

a

b

ARISTIDA ARIZONICA, *Vasey*.

ARISTIDA DIVARICATA H. B. K.

Rootstocks not seen. Roots rather stout, branching only below.

Culms tufted, erect, branching only at the base, 1 to 3 feet high, minutely re-trosely scabrous, simple, most of its length taken up by the panicle.

Leaves few, those of the stem 3 to 5; sheaths glabrous or minutely scabrous, imbricated, usually with a few long hairs at the apex; ligule a row of short hairs, with sometimes a few long ones intermixed; blades commonly 3 to 6 inches long, involute, usually glabrous beneath and scabrous above, never hairy. Root leaves similar, blades a little shorter.

Inflorescence paniculate. Panicle usually 9 to 18 inches long, frequently sheathed at the base; rachis nearly terete, glabrous; branches long (the lowest commonly 5 inches), widely spreading, naked at the base, flat, scabrous on the margins; spike-lets borne singly, mostly short-peduncled, and appressed to the branches.

Spikelets linear-subulate about 6 lines long (excluding the awns), somewhat compressed.

Glumes 3; first and second nearly equal, slightly spreading, narrowly linear, acute, membranaceous, tawny and purple in color, compressed, 1-nerved, nerve scabrous on the back; third (flowering) coriaceous, closely involute into a slender-cylindrical tube, scabrous above, slightly shorter than the empty glumes, scarcely twisted at the apex, produced into 3 straight, terete, scabrous, awns slightly diverging when dry, two lateral ones about as long as the body of the glume, middle one from one-half to twice longer. Rachilla elongated, between second and third glumes, to the length of $\frac{1}{2}$ line, densely short-villous.

Flower single, hermaphrodite. Palet minute, lanceolate, $\frac{1}{4}$ line long. Lodicules 2, shorter than the palet, linear-oblong. Stamens 3; anthers linear, $\frac{3}{4}$ line long. Stigmas 2, cylindrical.

Grain about 4 lines long, awl-shaped, tightly clasped by the flowering glume. Rachilla disarticulating above the second glume.

PLATE XXIII; *a*, spikelet, glumes spread apart and rhachilla separated at its point of disarticulation. The hairs on the apex of the sheaths are not shown, nor those on the rachilla above the second glume. The diameter of the tube of the flowering glume is often nearly twice as great.

Grows on dry or sandy hills and plains, extending to southern California.

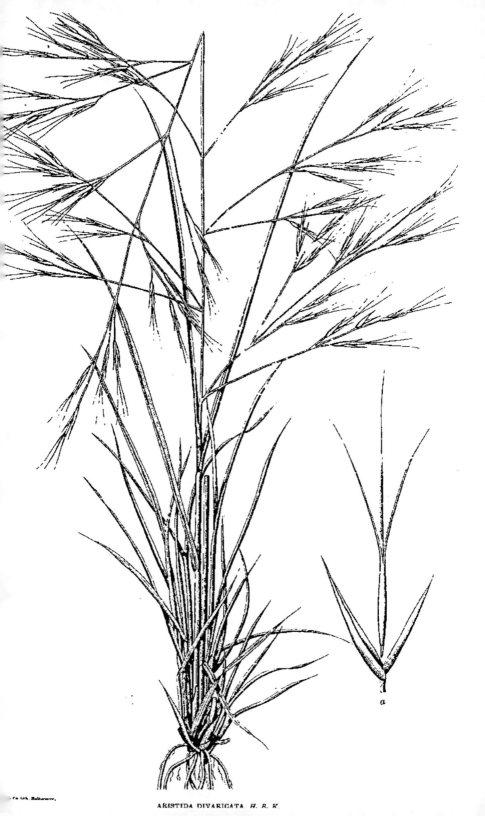

ARISTIDA DIVARICATA. *H. B. K.*

STIPA FLEXUOSA Vasey.

Culms closely set on a short horizontal rootstock with slender roots, erect, 1½ to 3 feet high, slender, terete, smooth, unbranched.

Leaves of the stem 2 to 4; sheaths smooth, close, usually imbricated; blades about 1 line broad, a few inches to 1 foot long, involute or the upper flat, glabrous on the back, minutely pubescent on the upper surface, hairy at the angle of the ligule; ligules membranaceous, 1 to 2 lines long, lacerate when old, broader than the blade.

Inflorescence paniculate. Panicle 6 to 12 inches long, erect; rachis slender, terete, glabrous; branches slender, flexuous, few-angled, scabrous, bearing towards the apex a few pedicelled spikelets.

Spikelets single, 1-flowered, on pedicels about 2 lines long, lanceolate, awl-shaped when closed, 6 to 9 lines long exclusive of the awn.

Glumes 3; first narrowly lanceolate, acute, membranaceous; glabrous, 1-nerved or with 2 lateral nerves at the base, hyaline above, green or purple below, as long as the spikelet; second similar, about one-fifth shorter, 3- to 5-nerved; third (flowering) about 2½ lines long closely involute about the flower into an awl-shaped terete body, villous on the outside, coriaceous at maturity, 5-nerved apex produced into a slender scabrous awn twisted in a right-handed spiral for about 5 lines, then bent, then twisted as before for about 3½ lines, then bent, and above the second bend not twisted. Rachilla elongated between the second and third glumes to the length of ¾ line, villous.

Flower hermaphrodite. Palet about one-third the length of the glume, oblong, obtuse, hyaline. Stamens 3; anthers linear, 1 to 1½ lines long, apex of each cell of the anther bearing a small tuft of hairs. Stigmas rather short, oblong.

Grain awl-shaped, about 2 lines long, inclosed in the glume, rachilla disarticulating just above the second glume, detached portion ending in a sharp point.

PLATE XXIV; *a*, and *b*, spikelet, the parts spread open and the upper portions of the rachilla detached at the point of disarticulation. The figure does not show the regular bends in the awn, nor the tufts of hairs at the apex of the anther cells.

This is more slender than *S. avenacea*, with smaller flowers, the flowering glume pubescent throughout, and the apex crowned with a row of white hairs.

STIPA PLUMOSA. Trem.

MUHLENBERGIA DISTICHOPHYLLA Kunth.

Rootstock not seen. Roots strong, branching rather early.

Culms tufted, erect, 2½ to 4 feet high, simple, glabrous, glaucous where not sheathed, stout, rigid.

Leaves of the stem 2 to 4; sheaths long, usually imbricated, not hairy, commonly minutely roughened; blade 3 to 12 inches long, about 1 line wide, flat and keeled or conduplicate, harsh, scabrous on the midrib and margins, glaucous green; ligule membranaceous, narrow, long-acuminate, sometimes ¾ inch long, fragile. Root leaves with sheaths mostly loose and compressed; sheaths sometimes 9 inches long, and the entire leaf exceeding 3 feet.

Inflorescence paniculate. Panicle 8 to 18 inches long, erect, contracted; branches numerous, seldom exceeding 3 inches, scabrous as well as the rachis.

Spikelets polygamous, very numerous, borne singly on slender scabrous pedicels, about 1 line long, linear-oblong, obtuse or acute.

Glumes 3; first and second nearly equal, membranaceous, tawny, often purple at the base, about 1 line long, slightly scabrous on the back, acute, or sometimes obtuse and erose at the apex, 1-nerved, rarely with 2 rudimentary lateral nerves; third (flowering) similar to the others, densely pilose below, with a strong middle nerve and usually 2 indistinct ones on either side; middle nerve in the hermaphrodite spikelets produced, from below the apex of the glume, into a slender, scabrous, terete, somewhat flexuous, purple awn 4 to 6 lines long; glume of the staminate spikelets awnless.

Flowers single in the spikelets. Palet of staminate flower thin, membranaceous, lanceolate, with 2 very slender approximate nerves, slightly hairy on the back; stamens 3, anthers linear, nearly as long as the spikelets. Palet of hermaphrodite flower similar to the other; stamens 3, anthers linear, nearly as long as the spikelet; ovary globular, styles long, stamens cylindrical.

Grain linear-oblong, brown, inclosed in the glume and palet; rachilla disarticulating above the second glume.

PLATE XXV; 1, male plant; 2, hemaphrodite plant; *a*, staminate spikelet; *b*, first and second glumes of the same; *c*, third (flowering) glume, palet, and stamens of the same; *f*, hermaphrodite flower; *d*, first and second glumes of the same; *e*, third (flowering) glume, palet, and stigmas of the same. In the hermaphrodite flower the stamens are not shown.

A coarse, strongly rooted, perennial grass, perhaps having agricultural value. It is one of the grasses called saccato.

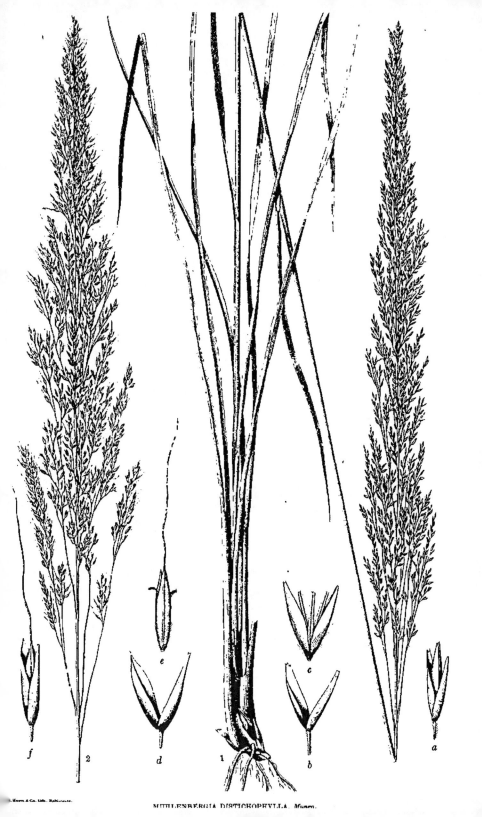

MUHLENBERGIA DISTICHOPHYLLA. *Munro.*

No. 26.

MUHLENBERGIA GRACILIS Trinius.

Rootstocks short, ascending.

Culms tufted, erect, 9 to 24 inches high, unbranched above the base, glabrous.

Leaves all radical; sheaths of the outer ones short (1 to 3 inches long), loose, flattened, slightly scabrous on the back, inner longer and sheathing, uppermost usually reaching to, and sheathing, the inflorescence; blade 6 inches or less long, in line with the sheaths, usually involute, scabrous on the back, glabrous above; ligule membranaceous, about ¼ to ½ inch long, at the base broader than the blade, apex slender-acute and often lacerate, the whole shriveled when old.

Inflorescence paniculate. Panicle sheathed or long-pedunculate, 2 to 7 inches long, erect or nearly so; rachis scabrous; branches scabrous, 2 inches long or less, nearly erect.

Spikelets lanceolate, acute, 2 lines long exclusive of the awn, borne singly on short pedicels.

Glumes 3; first lanceolate, acuminate-aristate, 1-nerved, scabrous on the back, about 1 line long, lead-colored below, hyaline above; second slightly longer, similar in texture, scabrous on the back, ovate-oblong, truncate, 3-nerved, nerves produced into aristate points; third (flowering) lanceolate, involute, 1-nerved or with two additional nearly marginal nerves, scabrous on the back, ciliate on the margins, as long as the spikelets, straw-colored, with a lead-colored apex tapering into a not twisted slender, scabrous, flexuous awn about ½ inch long.

Flower single, hermaphrodite. Palet lanceolate, slightly shorter than its glume, obtuse when flattened, 2-nerved, scabrous on the back. Stamens 3; anthers linear, about 1 line long. Stigmas cylindrical, purple.

Grain not seen. Palet and glume coriaceous when old.

PLATE XXVI; *a* and *b*, spikelet, the parts spread open, and the rachilla broken above the second glume; *c*, second glume; *d*, first glume; *e*, same as *b*, showing the back of the flowering glume.

This species is common on stony ridges or hills from Mexico to Montana, and a small form occurs in California.

MUHLENBERGIA GRACILIS, *Trin.*

EPICAMPES MACROURA Bentham.

Rootstock ascending, thick. Roots strong, little branched.
Culms tufted, erect, 2½ to 3½ feet high, glabrous, simple.

Leaves of the root several; sheaths mostly loose above and involute, 6 to 9 inches long, glabrous ; blade inserted on the back of the sheath, erect, commonly 1 foot long, glabrous, usually involute; ligule 3 to 6 lines long, lanceolate, coriaceous below, membranaceous above and on the margins, broader than the blade, appearing as a direct continuation of the sheath. Leaves of the stem 2 to 3, similar to those of the root; sheaths imbricated and mostly clasping ; blade frequently much shorter.

Inflorescence paniculate. Panicle short-pedunculate, erect, usually 8 to 16 inches long ; rachis terete, scabrous, branches imbricated, 1 to 4 inches long, nearly erect, scabrous, bearing the spikelets singly on short scabrous pedicels.

Spikelets nearly terete, lanceolate and acute when closed, about 1 line long.

Glumes 3; first and second nearly equal, two-thirds the length of the spikelet, oblong-lanceolate, acute or acuminate, 1-nerved, scabrous on the back ; third (flowering) similar in texture, a little longer, oblong, obtuse and bifid at the apex, with a short scabrous awn or mucro from the angle, 3- to 5-nerved, scabrous on the back.

Flowers single, hermaphrodite. Palet equaling the third glume, oblong, obtuse, 2-nerved, rarely scabrous. Stamens 3; anther linear, ¾ to 1 line long. Styles distinct, short; stigmas about half the length of the anthers, oblong, the fimbriæ long.

Grain dark brown, linear-oblong, obtuse or acutish at base and apex, terete, inclosed in the flowering glume and palet; rachilla disarticulating above the second glume.

PLATE XXVII ; *a*, first (on the right) and second glume ; *b*, flowering glume (on the right) and palet, open to show the stamens and pistil. The styles are much too long, while the stigmas should be twice as long and nearly four times broader.

This is another of the grasses called saccato, or saccatone.

EPICAMPES MACROURA, *Benth.*

No. 28.

EPICAMPES RIGENS Bentham.

Rootstocks rather slender, ascending. Roots rather stout, little branched. *Stems* tufted, erect, commonly 2 to 6 feet high, glabrous, simple. Leaves of the root few; sheath glabrous or slightly scabrous above, usually clasping, seldom exceeding 5˙inches in length; blade elongated, often exceeding 1 foot, usually involute, scabrous; ligule about 1 line long, truncate, margin minutely ciliate. Leaves of the stem 2 to 4, similar; sheaths mostly long and imbricated, often exceeding 1 foot.

Inflorescence paniculate. Panicle spike-like, 6 to 12 inches long, commonly ¼ to ⅜ inch in diameter, usually sheathed at the base; branches 1 inch long or less, appressed to the terete scabrous rachis. Branches and pedicels scabrous.

Spikelets lanceolate, narrowed at the base, terete, acute at the apex, 1½ to 2 lines long, borne singly on the pedicels, rachilla pilose between the second and third glumes.

Glumes 3; first and second nearly equal, lanceolate-oblong, obtuse or acute, 1-nerved, scabrous, two-thirds the length of the spikelet; third (flowering) broadly lanceolate when spread open, acute, 3- to 5-nerved, scabrous, with neither awn or mucro, hyaline below, usually lead-colored above.

Flower hermaphrodite, single. Palet lanceolate, equaling its glume, 2-nerved, acute at the apex. Stamens 3; anthers linear, about 1 line long. Stigmas short, long-fimbriate.

Grain not seen. Rachilla probably disarticulating above the second glume.

PLATE XXVIII; *a* and *b*, spikelet, opened and the parts separated; *c*, same, closed and facing in the opposite direction. The ovary is more than five times too long, and was probably drawn from a half matured specimen.

This is a coarse grass growing in dense clumps, and is also sometimes called saccato. It does not extend far northward.

EPICAMPES RIGENS, *Benth.*

CHLORIS ALBA Presl.

Plant annual.

Root slender, numerous.

Culms branching from the base and lower axils, procumbent at the base, rarely rooting at the lower nodes, glabrous, commonly 1½ to 3 feet high, often less.

Leaves 4 to 8 on the stem; sheaths glabrous, more or less bladdery-inflated, often loose, usually not contiguous; blades 1 to 2½ lines broad, 9 inches long or much shorter, flat, glabrous beneath, scabrous on the margins and above.

Inflorescence a sheathed or pedunculate cluster of sessile spikes. Spikes 5 to 15, 2 to 3½ inches long, only slightly spreading; rachis filiform, terete, straight, scabrous; spikelets closely set, sessile, in 2 rows along one side.

Spikelets compressed, 2-flowered; lower flower hermaphrodite; upper staminate or reduced to a sterile glume, 1¼ to 2 lines long (exclusive of awns and hairs).

Glumes 4; first one-third to one-half the length of the spikelet, lanceolate, acute or obtuse, membranaceous, 1-nerved, nerve scabrous; second about two-thirds the length of the spikelet, lanceolate, acute, membranaceous, its single nerve scabrous and produced into an aristate point nearly reaching the apex of the spikelet; rachilla pilose between the second and third glumes; third (flowering) obovate, compressed, apex narrowed making the glume hooded, pilose in irregular areas on the back, or glabrous, the margin short-pilose below, and on either margin near the apex long-pilose, hairs two-thirds as long as the spikelet, apex of the glume produced into a slender, scabrous, straight, not twisted awn two to three times the length of the spikelet; sterile glume similar in shape to the flowering glume, but smaller and glabrous, with a nearly equal awn. Rudiment of a third flower sometimes present.

Flower hermaphrodite. Palet oblanceolate, 2-nerved, margins folded inward. Stamens 3; anthers small, sagittate-lanceolate, ¼ line long; stigmas small, cylindrical. Flower of sterile glume sometimes wanting, sometimes represented only by a palet, rarely by stamens also.

Grain narrowly fusiform, acute at both ends, ¾ to 1 line long, inclosed in the flowering glume, the rachilla disarticulating above the second glume.

PLATE XXIX; *a* and *b*, spikelet, rachilla broken at the point of disarticulation, and the parts spread open. In *a* the shorter glume should be on the right and below, the longer on the left. In *b*, the sterile glume and the rudiments of a third flowering glume are shown.

This species is common in the southern parts of this region, and still more common in Mexico.

CHLORIS ALBA, Presl.

CHLORIS CILIATA Swartz, var. TEXANA Vasey n. var.

Plant annual.

Culms tufted, erect, compressed, glabrous, branching only at the base.

Leaves of the stem 3 to 5; sheaths not contiguous, glábrous, conspicuously striate, rarely loose; blades 1 to 2½ lines wide, 9 inches or less long, flat or sometimes involute, scabrous on the margins.

Inflorescence a short-pedunculate cluster of 4 to 6 sessile spikes. Spikes 2½ to 3½ inches long, slightly spreading; spikelets in 2 rows along one side of the slender scabrous rachis, inserted in each row at intervals of about ⅔ line.

Spikelets 1 to 1¼ lines long, truncate-cuneate, compressed.

Glumes 4; first and second lanceolate-oblong, acute, 1-nerved (nerves scabrous on the back) first about one-half the length of the spikelet, second nearly as long as the spikelet and with a short scabrous point; third (flowering) glume very broadly oblong, acute, 3-nerved (2 lateral nerves nearly marginate), sharply folded down the middle, densely long-pilose on the median nerve and on the middle third of the marginal nerves, bearing below the apex a short straight scabrous awn about one-half the length of the spikelet; fourth (sterile) glume broadly truncate-cuneate, 3-nerved, glabrous, folded down the middle, awned like the flowering glume. 2 or 3 additional successively smaller rudiments of glumes, of similar shape but unawned, often present. Rachilla short-pilose between the second and third glumes.

Flower single, hermaphrodite. Palet ovate, acute, 2-nerved, margins folded inward, nerves ciliate, body of the palet curved inward transversely and outward longitudinally. Stamens 3; anthers ovate-sagittate, ¼ line long. Stigmas cylindrical.

Grain not seen. Rachilla when mature disarticulating above the second glume.

PLATE XXX; *a*, spikelet; *b* and *c*, same, with the parts spread open and the rachilla broken at the point of disarticulation.

This variety (?) differs conspicuously from the type in the longer spikes; but we lack authentic specimens for comparison. It was collected near Brownsville, Texas, and probably is not found far from the coast.

CHLORIS CILIATA, *Swartz, Var.*

CHLORIS CUCULLATA Bischoff.

Plant annual.

Culms erect, at the base procumbent, 9 to 24 inches high, somewhat compressed or nearly terete, glabrous, branched only at the base.

Leaves of the root numerous; sheaths 3 inches long or less, glabrous, compressed, glaucous, with conspicuous membranaceous margins, the outer loose; blades 1 to 9 inches long, ¾ to 1½ lines wide, usually longitudinally folded, glaucous, scabrous on the midrib margins and upper surface, apex abruptly acute or mucronate; ligule about ½ line long, membranaceous, minutely ciliate at the apex. Leaves of the stem 2 to 4, similar to those of the root; sheaths not contiguous, upper more or less inflated; blade of the uppermost leaf often very small.

Inflorescence a more or less long-peduncled cluster of sessile spikes. Spikes 7 to 16, 1 to 2 inches long; spikelets borne in 2 rows along one side of the slender, scabrous rachis, inserted in each row at intervals of about ⅔ line.

Spikelet slightly less than 1 line long, of the form of an equilateral triangle.

Glumes 4; first and second oblong-lanceolate, hyaline, 1-nerved, nerve green and usually glabrous, apex acute or obtuse, first about ⅓ line long, second ½ to ⅔ line; third (flowering) glume compressed, 3-nerved, short-ciliate on the keel and intramarginal nerves, otherwise glabrous, bearing below the apex a minute scabrous awn ½ line long, each half of the glume oval, bluntly acute at either end; fourth (sterile) glume compressed, glabrous, awned similarly to the third, 5- to 7-nerved, the lateral nerves distant from the middle nerve, each half of the glume wedge-truncate, as broad as long, apex and free margin involute. Rudiment of a fifth glume usually present.

Flower single, hermaphrodite. Palet oval, 2-nerved, apex broadly notched, nerves ciliate, intramarginal, the narrow margins inflexed. Stamens 3; anthers ovate, sagittate, minute. Stigmas short, cylindrical.

Grain oblong, acute at both ends, loosely inclosed in its glume and palet, upper portion of the spikelet falling away together, rachilla disarticulating above the second glume.

PLATE XXXI; *a* and *b*, spikelet, the parts opened and the rachilla broken at the point of disarticulation. The flowering glume (to the left in *b*) should be ciliate on the back and the awn scabrous. The sterile glume (on the right in *b*) should be similarly awned, and the palet should be ciliate on the margins.

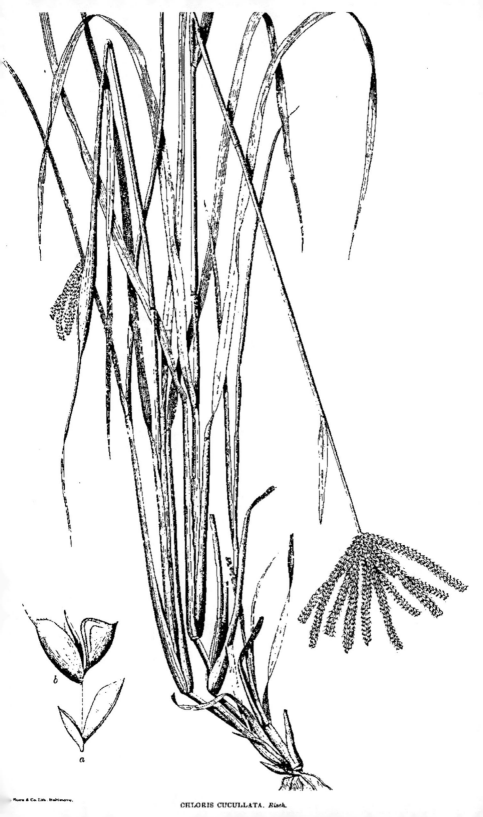

No. 32.

CHLORIS GLAUCA Vasey.

Plant annual, entirely glabrous.

Culm single, erect, 2 to 4 feet high, glabrous, unbranched.

Leaves of the root numerous; sheath very closely compressed, equitant, widely diverging, about 3 lines wide when folded, 8 inches or less long, continuing into the blade with a mere slight contraction at the mouth; blade folded below, flat above, keeled, 3 to 4 lines wide, 4 to 12 inches long, abruptly obtuse at the apex; second, third, and usually fourth internodes of the culm very short, their leaves similar to those of the root and appearing to start from the first node of the stem. Succeeding leaves 1 or 2, with longer close sheaths; blade nearly wanting.

Inflorescence an erect, pedunculate, umbellate cluster of 8 to 15 spikes. Spikes 3 to 5 inches long; rachis triangular, scabrous; this and the first and second glumes greenish straw-color, remainder of the spikelets very dark brown or black.

Spikelets in 2 rows on one side of the rachis, inserted alternately, those in each row at intervals of about ½ line, 1 line long.

Glumes 4; first ⅔ line long, ovate-lanceolate, acute, inæquilateral, with 1 rigid scabrous nerve; second 1 line long, linear, notched at the apex, nerved like the first, nerve produced into a short deflexed scabrous mucro, mucros second along the edge of the spike; third (flowering) glume compressed, scabrous toward the apex, each half oblong, acute; fourth (sterile) glume obovate, truncate, scabrous along the upper margin, rolled into a tube.

Flower single, hermaphrodite. Palet oblanceolate-oblong, notched at the acute apex, 2-nerved, with additional inflexed membranaceous margins. Stamens 3; anthers oblong-linear, ¼ line long, notched at the apex. Stigmas short cylindrical.

Grain oblong, acute at either end, triangular in cross-section; rachilla disarticulating above the second glume.

Plate XXXII; *a* and *b*, spikelet opened to show the parts; rachilla broken at the point of disarticulation. The leaf belonging to the uppermost node of the stem is not shown.

NOTE.—This species was inserted here, by mistake, instead of *Chloris Swartziana* Doell. (*Chloris petræa* Swz.), which occurs in Texas near the coast. It is much less robust, with narrower leaves, fewer spikes (3 to 5), and some difference in the flowers. It is possible, however, that both species may occur, although *Chloris glauca* is principally known from Florida.

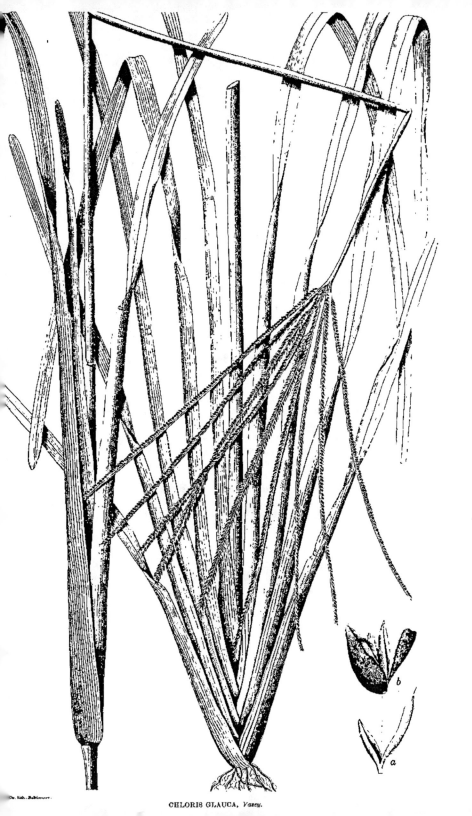

CHLORIS GLAUCA, Vasey.

CHLORIS VERTICILLATA Nuttall.

Plant annual.

Culms single or few in a tuft, 10 to 16 inches high, branching at the base, the branches commonly sterile, spreading below.

Leaves sometimes obtuse, but usually acuminate, at the apex; sheath provided at the throat, especially near the margin within, with a few long slender hairs.

Inflorescence short-pedunculate or sometimes sheathed below. Spikes 8 to 14, 4 to 6 inches long, often naked at the base, clustered at the apex of the stem and at that point hairy, or a few verticillate branches in 1 or 2 series on a prolongation of the axis. Spikelets arranged in 2 rows on one side of the slender, scabrous rachis, at intervals in each row of about 2 to 2½ lines.

Spikelet about 1½ lines long, cuneate-obovate, compressed.

Glumes 4; first and second with 1 scabrous nerve, first as long as the spikelet, lanceolate, aristate-acute; second with a longer point, exceeding the spikelet; third (flowering) glume 3-nerved, bearing a slender scabrous awn (4 to 5 lines long) below the apex, broadly oblong, bluntly acute at each end, short-pilose on the midrib and intramarginal nerves, elsewhere glabrous; fourth (sterile) glume broadly obovate, nearly truncate, 3-nerved, glabrous, with an awn 3 to 4 lines long; small fifth glume, similar in form to fourth, usually present.

Flower sometimes single, hermaphrodite. Palet narrowly oblong, 2-nerved, nerves ciliate and margins inflexed. Stames 3; anthers minute. Stigmas cylindrical. Flower often present in the axil of the fourth glume, sometimes hermaphrodite, sometimes reduced to an empty palet.

Grain not seen.

PLATE XXXIII; *a*, spikelet opened to show the parts, the rachis broken. The figure represents an unexpanded panicle; when expanded, the branches are spread at right angles with the axis.

CHLORIS VERTICILLATA, *Nutt.*

No. 34.

BOUTELOUA.

The genus *Bouteloua*, which includes those grasses popularly called grama grass, is a very large one in the Southwest, embracing many species, both annuals and perennials. They are nearly all nutritious and valuable for pasturage. The general characters of the inflorescence are as follows: 1 or several-flowered spikes single at the apex of the culm, or several disposed in a raceme; these spikes closely crowded or loosely imbricated with spikelets arranged on one side of the rachis in 2 rows; spikelets usually consisting of 1 perfect flower and a pedicel (bearing 1 to 3 stiff awns, and usually a few imperfect glumes with the awns); one or two additional imperfect flowers rarely present in the spikelet; flowering glumes variously lobed at the apex, lobes terminating with awns. The several species present a great diversity in the details of these general features.

BOUTELOUA ARENOSA Vasey.

Plant annual. Roots few, fibrous.

Culms in tufts, erect or decumbent, simple or geniculate and branching below, slender, 6 to 10 inches long.

Leaves sparse; sheath loose, shorter than the internode, striate; ligule conspicuous, strongly ciliate; blade ½ to 1 line wide, 1 to 2 inches long, long-acuminate.

Panicle 2 to 2½ inches long, composed of 3 or 4, mostly one-sided sessile spikes, ½ to ¾ inches long, erect, or somewhat recurved, consisting of about 20 spikelets arranged alternately on the narrow flattened rachis.

Spikelets imbricated, each with 1 perfect and 1 rudimentary flower, about 3 lines long including the awns.

Empty *glumes* thin, smooth, 1-nerved, oblong-lanceolate, 1 to 1½ lines long, upper usually the longer, both acute and sometimes toothed at the apex and terminated with a short awn; flowering glume woolly externally, dividing into 2 lateral and 1 central awn, body about 1 line long, extending into 2 narrow teeth or lobes rather shorter than the awns, lateral awns nearly 2 lines long, central one somewhat shorter.

Palet narrower than its glume, 2- to 4-toothed, 2-nerved, nerves extended into awns. Imperfect flower inclosed by the flowering glume, consisting of 3 long awns at the summit of a short hairy pedicel, 2 of the awns having each a rudimentary scale at the base.

PLATE XXXIV; *a*, spikelet enlarged; *b*, empty glumes; *c*, flowering glume; *d*, palet; *e*, imperfect flower.

The specimens were from loose sandy soil, at Guaymas on the Gulf of California.

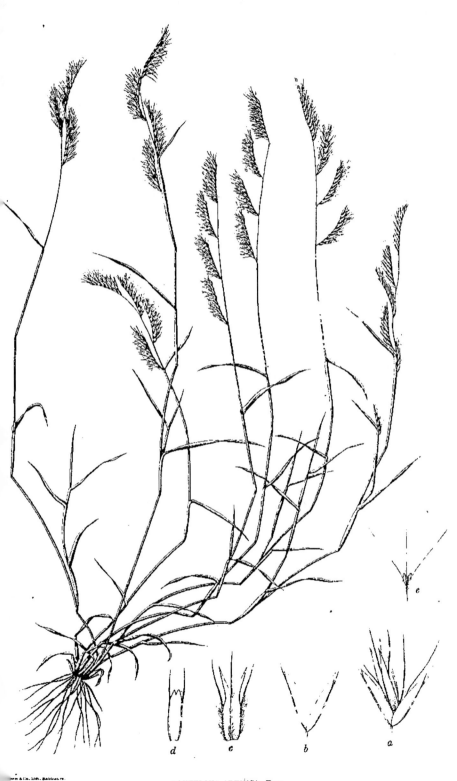

d   c   b   a

BOUTELOUA ARENOSA, *Vasey.*

BOUTELOUA ARISTIDOIDES Thurber.

Plant annual.

Culms erect or decumbent, frequently geniculate and branching, slender, growing in clusters, very variable in development, often fruiting when a few inches high, sometimes reaching 2 feet in height.

Leaves with blades varying with the size of the plant from 1 to 3 or 4 inches in length, very narrow, erect, finely pointed ; sheath short, striate, smooth except a few long hairs at the top; ligule a short, ciliate ring.

Panicles racemose, terminal and lateral, mostly 2 to 4 inches long, and consisting of 10 to 12 narrow, nearly sessile flower-spikes, these generally one-sided, in age spreading or horizontal, or even reflexed. Spikes ¼ to ¾ inch long, on short hairy pedicels ; each spike with 2 to 4 closely appressed spikelets, lowest without the imperfect flower and pedicel.

Spikelets 3 lines long.

Lower empty glume linear or awl-shaped, one-half as long as the stouter upper one ; this 3 lines long, 1-nerved, somewhat pubescent on the back ; flowering glume linear-lanceolate, acuminate, 3-nerved, 3-toothed at the apex.

Palet a little shorter, 2-nerved, 2-toothed. Rudimentary flower consisting of 3 long awns on a short pedicel, wanting in the lower spikelet.

PLATE XXXV; *a*, spike; *b*, empty glumes ; *c*, flowering glume; *d*, flowering glume of the lowest spikelet; *e*, palet ; *f*, rudiment.

This species springs up in great abundance after the summer rains, and for a short time furnishes a large amount of food for stock on the ranges. It is one of the so-called six-weeks grasses.

BOUTELOUA ARISTIDOIDES, *Thurb.*

No. 36.

BOUTELOUA BURKEI Scribner.

Rootstock short, strongly rooted, thickly covered with the crowded culms.
Culms slender, 4 to 8 inches high, with 3 to 4 nodes each.

Leaves mostly crowded at the base, small, $\frac{1}{2}$ to $1\frac{1}{2}$ inches long, $\frac{1}{4}$ line wide; ligule very short, ciliate; sheaths narrow, mostly shorter than the internodes.

Inflorescence racemose-spicate, about one-third the length of the plant, consisting of about 5 spikes horizontal or even reflexed in age. Spikes $\frac{1}{4}$ to $\frac{3}{4}$ inch long, of 10 to 15 spikelets, arranged in 2 rows on one side of the rachis. Spikelets about 3 lines long including the awns.

Empty *glumes* 2, lanceolate, 1-nerved, smooth, nearly equal; body of the flowering glume less than 1 line long, nearly as broad, pubescent on the back, dividing into 3 lobes extended into awns;

Palet narrow, 2-nerved, 2-dentate at apex; imperfect flower consisting of 3 awns on a short, smooth pedicel.

PLATE XXXVI; *a*, spike; *b*, spikelet; *c*, empty glumes; *d*, flowering glume; *e*, palet; *f*, imperfect flower.

This species is closely related to *B. trifida*, which is somewhat larger, the empty glumes narrower and unequal, and the flowering glume longer and smooth.

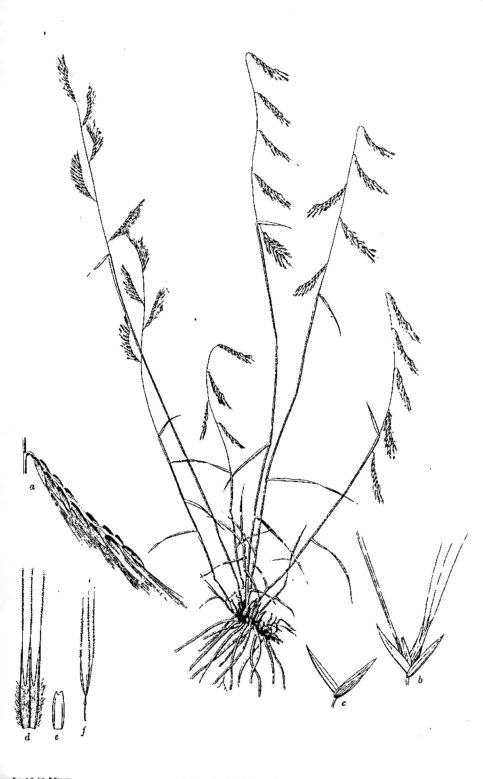

BOUTELOUA BURKEI, *Scrib.*

BOUTELOUA ERIOPODA Torrey.

Perennial, strongly rooted.

Culms rather weak, straggling, often decumbent and rooting at the lower joints, 1 to 3 feet long, lower part of the culm and sheaths woolly-pubescent, particularly near the roots.

Leaves of the stem 5 or 6; blades narrow, short, 2 to 3 inches long, 1 to 2 lines wide, or from proliferous shoots, sometimes from 4 to 6 inches long; sheaths much shorter than the internodes.

Panicle racemose, 3 to 6 inches long, composed of 5 or 6 one-sided nearly sessile spikes; these 1 to 2 inches long, erect-spreading, each containing 15 to 20 spikelets.

Spikelets each with 1 perfect and 1 imperfect flower, 4 to 5 lines long, including the awns.

Perfect flower: outer empty glumes lanceolate, acuminate, 1-nerved, very unequal, lower about one-half the length of the upper; flowering glume pubescent at the base, otherwise smooth, faintly 3-nerved, linear-oblong, 3 lines long, with 2 narrow teeth at the apex and a middle one prolonged into an awn 1 line long; palet nearly as long, narrower, 2-nerved, finely 2-toothed at the apex.

Imperfect flower consisting of 3 slender awns on a pedicel, with a narrow tuft of hair below the united awns; whole 4 to 5 lines long.

PLATE XXXVII: 1, plant of matured size; 2, panicle of a smaller plant; *a*, empty glumes; *b*, flowering glume, palet, stamens, pistil, and imperfect flower.

This is the common black grama grass of southern New Mexico and Arizona, and is the most valuable grass of the mesas.

BOUTELOUA HAVARDII Vasey.

Rootstock short, roots very strong.

Culms erect, 1 to 2 foot high, leafy at the base, sparsely leafy above.

Lower *leaves* with the blades crowded, concave, rigid, rough on the margins and beneath, ciliate with short, rather distant, hairs; lower sheaths short, loose, striate; ligule a ring of short hairs; upper sheaths becoming much longer, blades shorter.

Panicle 1½ to 2½ inches long, composed of 5 to 7 short, thickish, approximate spikes, with short, woolly pedicels; spikes about ½ inch long, erect or spreading, consisting of 9 to 13 crowded spikelets on a hairy rachis.

Spikelets 3 inches long beside the awns of the sterile flower, hairy.

Empty *glumes* lanceolate, acuminate, unequal; upper one 3 lines long, with a thick midrib, pungent, twice as long as the lower, both beset on the back with long white hairs; flowering glumes oblong-lanceolate, 3-nerved, 3 lines long, 3-toothed at the apex, strongly ciliate on the margins.

Palet about as long as its glume, 2-nerved, 2-toothed at the apex. Imperfect flower composed of 3 stout awns, 5 to 6 lines long, these hairy below and united at the summit of a naked pedicel.

PLATE XXXVIII: *a*, spikelet; *b*, flowering glume; *c*, palet; *d*, imperfect flower.

BOUTELOUA HAVARDII, *Vasey.*

BOUTELOUA HIRSUTA Lagasca.

Roots fibrous, cæspitose.

Culms erect, simple, or in var. *minor* geniculate and branching below.

Leaves usually short, 1 to 4 inches long, narrow, sometimes ciliate on the margins, produced into a long, fine point; lower sheaths short, upper longer, and with shorter blades.

Panicle consisting of from 1 to 3 erect spikes, ½ to 1¼ inches long.

Spikelets about 3 lines long, hirsute, densely crowded on one side of the smooth rachis; this extended in a naked point beyond the flowers.

Empty *glumes* unequal, lower about 1 line in length, narrowly lanceolate, acute, smooth; upper about 2½ lines long, lanceolate, acuminate, awn-pointed, with a row of dark or black glands on either side of the midrib, each one emitting a long hair; flowering glume 2¼ lines long, including the awns, nearly smooth, oblong, lower half entire, upper divided into 3 lobes, each terminating in a short awn.

Palet narrower, entire, 2-nerved.

Imperfect flower on a short, smooth pedicel, consisting of 3 awns and 3 scales, awns extending a little beyond the perfect flower.

PLATE XXXIX: 1, typical plant; 2, var. *minor;* 3, var. *major;* a, empty glumes; b, perfect and imperfect flowers; c, flowering glume.

Several forms are grouped under this species; the three principal ones being here illustrated. The species has a wide range, from Mexico northward to Montana and east of the Mississippi in Illinois and Wisconsin. It is by no means as plentiful as *B. oligostachya,* and is less valuable as a forage grass.

BOUTELOUA HIRSUTA Lag.

No. 40.

BOUTELOUA HUMBOLDTIANA Kunth.

Culms erect, rarely branching, firm, 15 to 20 inches high, smooth, leafy below.

Leaves: sheath open, striate, shorter than the internodes; ligule inconspicuous; blade 1 to 2 lines wide, 3 to 6 inches long, scabrous especially on the margins, often sparsely ciliate below.

Inflorescence racemose, 3 to 4 inches long, consisting of about 7 to 9 one-sided, short-pedicelled spikes, lower ones ½ inch or more distant, others gradually shorter; spikes about ½ inch long, each consisting of 7 to 9 smooth spikelets, somewhat loosely overlapping each other.

Spikelets about ¼ inch long, including the awns, smooth, consisting of 2 to 3 flowers, upper male, others perfect, or the lower 2 fertile and the upper reduced to an awn.

Empty *glumes* nearly equal, 3 to 4 lines long, keeled, lanceolate, acute; flowering glume of the lower flower 4 lines long, lanceolate, 3-nerved, 3-toothed, at the apex of the second flower similar, but with the teeth extended into long awns (2 to 3 lines long).

Palet nearly as long as the glume, 2-nerved, 2-toothed at the apex. Third flower when present, sometimes with awns still longer, or imperfect or reduced.

PLATE XL: *a*, spikelet; *b*, empty glumes; *c*, flowering glume of the fertile flower; *d*, palet of the fertile flower; *c'*, flowering glume of the second flower; *d'*, palet of the second flower. The sterile flower reduced to a small pedicel is seen in *a*.

It is doubtful whether this plant, which has passed under the name *B. Humboldtiana*, is really identical with that described by Kunth. Our plant is more probably a form of *B. bromoides* Lag. In range it seldom extends north of New Mexico.

a

b

c' *d'*

e *d*

BOUTELOUA OLIGOSTACHYA Torrey.

Culms cæspitose from a short thick rootstock extending into a thick close mat, slender, smooth, erect, 1 to 2 feet high.

Leaves mostly near the ground; blade short, curled, in moist situations becoming slender and longer, very narrow, attenuate into a slender point; sheath shorter than the internodes, close; ligule very short, ciliate.

Inflorescence consisting of 1 to 3 spikes, densely crowded with flowers on one side of the rachis, 1 to 1½ inches long, usually becoming curved and spreading; rachis narrow and sparsely pubescent.

Spikelets very numerous (often 50 or more), in 2 rows on one side of the rachis, nearly at right angles with it, sparsely pubescent, sometimes sparsely glandular on the keel, about 3 lines long, containing 1 perfect flower and 1 rudimentary one.

Empty *glumes* unequal, awn-pointed; lower one-half to two-thirds as long as the upper, thin; upper 2½ to 3 lines long, purplish; flowering glume lanceolate, 3 lines long, including the awns, hairy on the back, lobed to or nearly to the middle, middle lobe broad, lateral ones very narrow, all terminating in sharp awns.

Palet nearly equal in length to the flowering glume, narrower, 2-toothed at the apex, 2-nerved. Imperfect flower reduced to 3 equal awns, with 1 or 2 scales at the base, on a short pedicel having a tuft of white hairs at the top.

PLATE XLI: 1 and 2, typical plant; 3, larger form; *a*, empty glumes; *b*, perfect and imperfect flowers; *c*, flowering glume, from the back.

This species is probably more widely spread than any other of the family, and is the one which constitutes with the buffalo grass (*Buchloë dactyloides*) the main vegetation of the vast plains of the West.

BOUTELOUA OLIGOSTACHYA, Torr.

No. 42.

BOUTELOUA PROSTRATA Lagasca.

Annual. Roots fibrous.

Culms growing in small depressed tufts, spreading or decumbent, geniculate, leafy to the top.

Leaves with short narrow blades ½ to 1½ inches long; sheath somewhat loose, shorter than the internodes, striate; ligule inconspicuous.

Inflorescence a single terminal spike, generally recurved, ¾ to 1 inch long, smooth.

Spikelets 20 to 30, in rows on one side of the smooth rachis, nearly 3 lines long, containing 1 perfect and 2 imperfect flowers.

Empty *glumes* unequal; lower about one-half the length of the upper, narrow; upper about 2 lines long, ovate-lanceolate, acute; flowering glume smooth or slightly pubescent on the back, about 3 lines long, lower half broadly oblong, upper 3-lobed, 3-awned, middle lobe broadest and longest, awns stiff.

Palet nearly 2 lines long, denticulate at the apex. ¯ Imperfect flower reduced to 3 stiff awns with 1 or 2 scales at the base. on a short pedicel having a tuft of white hairs at the top.

PLATE XLII: *a*, spikelet; *b*, empty glumes; *c*, flowering glume from the back; *d*, palet; *e*, imperfect flower.

This annual grass is widely distributed from Mexico to Colorado, prevailing in bottom lands, where it frequently mats the ground, but does not seem to be relished by cattle.

BOUTELOUA PROSTRATA, *Lag.*

No. 43.

BOUTELOUA RACEMOSA Lagasca.

Culms in close tufts from a strongly rooted rootstock 2 to 3 feet high, unbranched.

Leaves with blades 4 to 12 inches long, 2 lines wide, long-pointed, scabrous; sheath loose, sparsely pubescent; ligule short.

Inflorescence racemose, 6 to 9 inches long, composed of 20 to 40 alternate, sometimes one-sided, short-pedicelled or nearly sessile, short spikes, these spreading or recurved, sometimes approximate, sometimes rather distant; common rachis angular, scabrous.

Spikes ⅓ to ½ inch long, variable in thickness and fullness, usually of about 5 spikelets, sometimes reduced to 2 or 3.

Spikelets 2 to 3 lines long without the awns, each 2-flowered.

Empty *glumes* unequal; lowest one-third shorter than the upper, narrow, awn-pointed; upper 2 lines long or more, ovate-lanceolate, acute; flowering glume about 2 lines long, oblong, smooth or somewhat pubescent on the margins, 3-nerved near the apex, with 3 short arms.

Palet as long as its glume, 2-nerved, 2-toothed at apex. Imperfect flower varying in development from a few rudimentary awns to a nearly full-formed flower, or in var. *aristosa* having a long-awned flowering glume and rudimentary scales.

PLATE XLIII: above, spike of about 3 spikelets; below, flower showing the empty glumes, perfect and imperfect flowers.

This is perhaps more widely diffused than any other species, ranging from Mexico to British America and east of the Mississippi in Illinois, Ohio, and several localities in eastern New York.

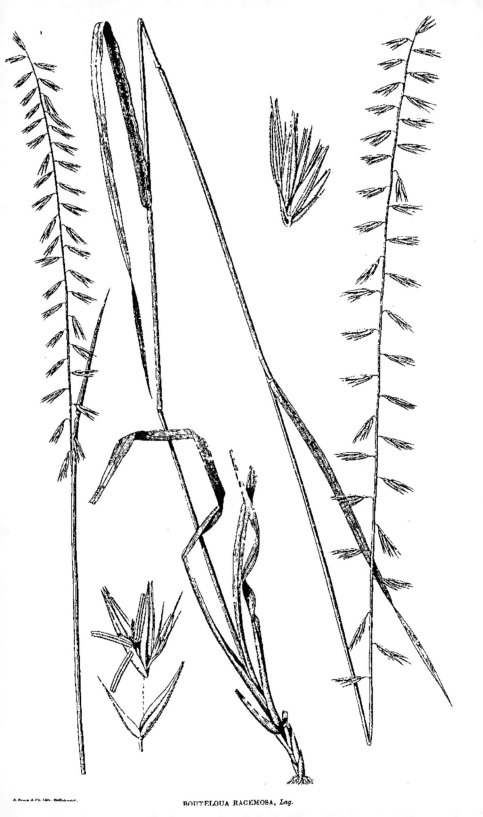

BOUTELOUA RAMOSA Scribner.

Culms many from a crowded short rootstock, strongly rooted, wiry-branched and almost woody below, slender, above leafy to the inflorescence, smooth.

Leaves with blades narrow, short, 1 to 2 inches long, attenuated to a fine point; sheath smooth, striate, with a few long hairs at the top; ligule very short.

Inflorescence consisting usually of 2 spikes, 1 to 1¼ inches apart at the apex of the culm, 1 to 1¼ inches long, crowded with the 20 to 30 one-sided spikelets.

Spikelets about 2½ lines long, with 1 perfect and 1 imperfect flower.

Empty *glumes* smooth, acute, unequal; lower less than one-half as long as the upper, narrow; upper lanceolate, nearly 2 lines long; flowering glumes over 2 lines long, lanceolate, clothed with long white hairs on the back and margins, divided at the apex into 3 sharply awned lobes.

Palet narrower, 2-toothed at the apex, smooth. Imperfect flower consisting of 3 awns with 2 or 3 imperfect glumes at their base, on a short pedicel densely hairy-tufted at the apex.

PLATE XLIV: *a*, spikelet spread open to show the parts; *b*, empty glumes; *c*, flowering glume; *d*, palet; *e*, imperfect or sterile flower and its pedicel.

This species extends from northern Mexico to Arizona and western Texas.

a *d* *c* *b* *e*

BOUTELOUA RAMOSA, *Scrib.*

No. 45.

BOUTELOUA STRICTA Vasey.

Culms 2 to 2½ foot high, unbranched, wiry, stiffly erect, smooth; base clothed with old, persistent, broad sheaths.

Leaves few; blade erect, rigid, narrow, becoming setaceous-involute, 4 to 6 inches long, scabrous on the upper surface; lower sheaths broad, loose, smooth, and short, upper becoming long and narrow (3 to 4 inches long); ligule very short, ciliate.

Inflorescence about 4 inches long, consisting of 5 or 6 erect or appressed, narrow, one-sided spikes, these ¾ to 1 inch long, densely crowded with the 30 to 50 spikelets.

Spikelets 2 lines long, including the awns.

Empty *glumes* unequal, lanceolate, acute; lower one-half as long as the upper, nearly smooth; flowering glume 2 lines long, pubescent externally, oblong-lanceolate, 3-lobed above, lobes awned, lateral lobes a little shorter than the the central one.

Palet narrow, nearly as long as its glume, 2-nerved, 2-toothed at the apex. Imperfect flower consisting of 3 equal awns, with 2 or 3 imperfect glumes at the base, on a short pedicel with a tuft of soft hairs at its apex.

PLATE XLV; *a*, spikelet; *b*, empty glumes; *c*, flowering glume, seen from the back; *d*, palet; *e*, imperfect flower.

This species differs from *B. oligostachya* in its more wiry culms, more rigid habit, setaceous, appressed leaves, and dense, appressed, and more numerous spikes.

d   b   a   c   e

BOUTELOUA STRICTA, *Vasey.*

No. 46.

BOUTELOUA TRIFIDA Thurber.

Culms 6 to 12 inches long, slender, numerous, crowded on a short rootstock; base often thickened, covered with short, broad sheaths.

Leaves; blades small, radical sometimes 2 or 3 inches long, those of the culm often reduced to ¼ inch, smooth or sparsely hairy; sheath shorter than the internode.

Inflorescence of 4 to 6 erect or somewhat spreading smooth spikes, with about 15 to 30 spikelets rather loosely disposed.

Spikelets 3 lines long including the awns, containing 1 perfect and 1 imperfect flower.

Empty *glumes* slightly unequal; upper 1½ lines long; lower one-fourth shorter, smooth, 1-nerved; flowering glumes narrow, body oblong, smooth, less than 1 line long, dividing above into 3 long-awned lobes (2 to 2½ lines long).

Palet somewhat shorter and narrower than its glume, 2-toothed at the apex. Imperfect flower reduced to 3 slender awns slightly enlarged toward the base, on a short, smooth pedicel.

PLATE XLVI; *a*, spikelet; *b*, empty glumes; *c*, flowering glume; *d*, palet; *e*, imperfect flower.

This species closely resembles *B. Burkei*, No. 36, but a close comparison shows important differences.

BOUTELOUA TRIFIDA. *Thurb.*

BUCHLOË DACTYLOIDES Engelmann.

Plant usually diœcious, rarely monœcious, male and female flowers hetero-morphous.

Culms low, 4 to 8 inches high, in dense matted tufts or patches, interlaced with stolons from a few inches to 2 feet long, with nodes usually 2 to 3 inches apart, these developing tufts of leaves and culms and often taking root.

MALE PLANT.

Culms slender, erect or decumbent at base, with 3 or 4 leaves.

Leaves. Radical 4 to 6 inches long, 1 line or less wide, acuminate, smooth or ciliate, those of the culm ½ to 2 inches long; upper sheaths often longer than the blades, loose; ligule and throat hairy.

Inflorescence a terminal panicle of 2 to 4 approximate, sessile or nearly sessile spikes, each ¼ inch or less in length.

Spikelets 5 to 10 or more in 2 ranks on one side of the rachis, crowded, each 2- or 3-flowered, about 2 lines long.

Outer empty *glumes* unequal, 1-nerved or the lower nerveless and minute, the upper one-half to two-thirds as long as the spikelet, oblong, acute, minutely pub-escent; flowering glumes ovate, 2 lines long, membranaceous.

Palet ovate, acuminate, as long as the flowering glumes, 2-nerved; stamens 3; anthers 1 line long, linear.

FEMALE PLANT.

Flowering culms short, 2 to 3 inches high, 2 or 3 upper leaves clustered at the apex, their sheaths inclosing the base of the fertile flowers.

Inflorescence consisting of 1 to 3, commonly 2, short, clustered spikes, each 3 to 3½ lines high, and of about 5 spikelets; rachis of the spike thickened.

Spikelets very different from the male ones, being each 1-flowered and the parts much indurated and modified.

Upper empty *glume* indurated and cohering at the base with the enlarged rachis, becoming almost woody, divided at the apex into 3 or more rigid teeth, body convex externally and infolding the flower on its concave side; all the lower empty glumes (except that of the lowest spikelet) thin, ovate, acute, 1-nerved, scale-like, on the inner side of the spikelet; flowering glumes coriaceous, 3-nerved, 3-toothed at apex.

Palet similar in texture to the flowering glume, 2-nerved, 2-toothed, inclosing the large ovary.

PLATE XLVII; 1, male plant; 2, female plant; *a*, male spikelets; *b*, empty glumes of same; *c*, flowering glume of same; *d*, palet of same; *A*, female spikelet; *B*, upper empty glume; *C*, flowering glume; *D*, palet.

This grass is extensively spread over all the region known as the Great Plains. It grows in extensive patches, spreading largely by means of its stolons (similar to those of Bermuda grass), which are sometimes 3 feet long, with joints every few inches, frequently rooting at the joints and forming new plants.

The flowers of the two sexes are usually on separate plants, but sometimes both kinds are found on different parts of the same plant. This and the grama grass (*Bouteloua oligostachya*) are the principal native grasses of the Plains, and afforded the principal subsistence of the herds of buffalo which formerly inhabited them. It is rapidly disappearing before the advance of settlements.

EREMOCHLOE BIGELOVII Watson.

AND

EREMOCHLOE KINGII Watson.

1. *Eremochloë Bigelovii.*

Culms 6 to 10 inches high, tufted, branching below, smooth; upper portion naked, except 2 or 3 small approximate leaves below the panicle.

Leaves with blades ½ to 1½ inches long, setaceous, striate, pungent.

Panicle small, 1 inch or less long, simple, or with 1 or 2 short branches, few-flowered.

Spikelets 4-flowered; 2 lower neutral; third perfect; fourth, or uppermost, reduced to 3 feathery awns on a short pedicel.

Empty glumes lanceolate, smooth, 1-nerved, about 3 lines long.

Sterile flowers consisting each of a flowering glume and palet. Flowering glume 2-lobed to the middle, densely ciliate, 3-nerved, with a slender feathery awn between the lobes, these tipped with a short awn; palets very narrow, smooth, 2-nerved, 2-toothed at the apex or very rudimentary.

Perfect flower with the flowering glume deeply 3-lobed, lobes extending into stiff ciliate awns; palet two-thirds as long, ovate, abruptly acuminate, smooth, slightly toothed at the apex; awns 3, strongly ciliate and united at the apex of a short smooth pedicel; a linear or awn-like scale sometimes attached to one of the sterile palets.

2. *Eremochloë Kingii.*

Culms low, tufted, 1 to 2 inches high.

Leaves crowded at the base of the stem; sheath dilated, ciliate at the margins and apex, persistent, and with the old blades cut into fibrillæ; blades ½ to 1 inch long, rigid, involute, pungent.

Panicle short, oblong, sheathed at the base by the upper leaf, less simple than in the other species.

Spikelet 4-flowered; flowers as in *E. Bigelovii.*

Empty glumes 4 lines long, acute, smooth.

Sterile flowers more deeply lobed; middle awn membranaceous, margined below.

Perfect flower with the flowering glume deeply 3-lobed, middle lobe narrower. Pedicel and awns similar.

PLATE XLVIII; 1, *Eremochloë Bigelovii; a*, empty glumes; *b*, flowering glume; *c*, palet; *d*, pedicel and feathery awns.

2, *Eremochloë Kingii; e*, spikelet; *f*, empty glumes; *g*, flowering glume: *h*, palet; *i*, pedicel and feathery awns.

Eremochloe Bigelovii was found on the bluffs of the Rio Grande in western Texas. It has not recently been collected.

E. Kingii has been found at Peach Springs, Arizona, and at several places in Nevada.

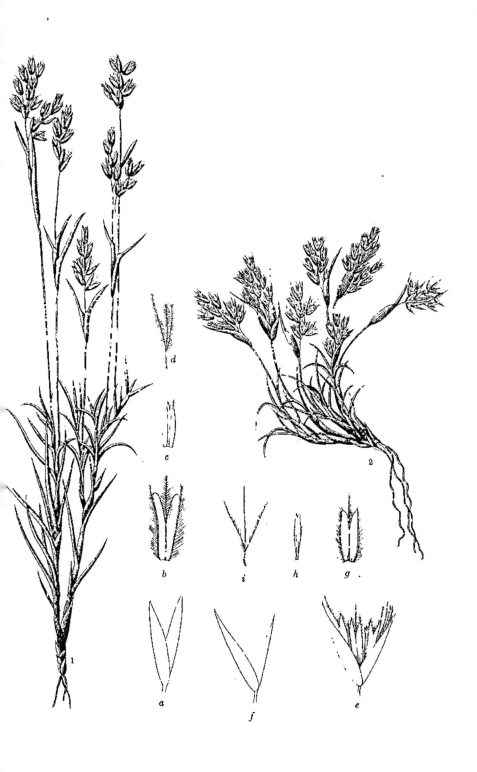

1 EREMOCHLOË BIGELOVII, S. W.   2 EREMOCHLOË KINGII, S. W.

MELICA DIFFUSA Pursh.

Plant perennial.

Rootstock not seen. Roots slender.

Culms usually single, simple, erect, 2 to 5 feet high, sometimes shorter, terete, glabrous.

Leaves of the stem 4 to 6; sheaths usually distant, closely sheathing, glabrous, margins grown together to within about ½ inch from the summit; blade 5 to 8 inches long, flat and reaching 4 lines broad, or much narrower (1½ lines) and involute, smooth or scabrous on both surfaces, scabrous points on the upper surface often producing hairs; ligule 1 to 2 lines long, lacerate when old.

Inflorescence paniculate. Panicle long-pedunculate, 4 to 10 inches long, with 3 to 7 nodes; branches 2 at each node, widely spreading, scabrous; one much the smaller, longer not exceeding 2½ inches; rachis terete, nearly scabrous. Spikelets single, on slender scabrous pedicels enlarged and villous at the apex, abruptly bent just below.

Spikelets narrowly to broadly oblong, slightly compressed, 4½ to 6 lines long, 2- to 4-flowered with rudiments of 1 or 2 others above.

Glumes with green nerved body and membranaceous margins and apex; first 5-nerved, 3 to 3½ lines long, oval, apex from broadly acute to acuminate; second about 5-nerved, 4 to 5 lines long, oblong-oblanceolate, apex broadly acute; flowering glume narrowly oblong, many-nerved, acute, scabrous on the back, 1 to 3 nerves passing through the membranaceous margin to the apex, lowest 4 to 5½ lines long, upper successively shorter.

Flowers hermaphrodite. Palet oblong-oblanceolate in position, ciliate on the 2 nerves above, acute, with additional inflexed margins. Stamens 3; anthers linear, about 1¼ lines long. Stigmas not seen.

Grain 1 line long, narrowly oblong, obtuse at both ends, loosely inclosed between the glume and palet (and dropping from them when mature?); outer coat loose, wrinkled, and shining.

PLATE LXIX; *a* and *b*, spikelet enlarged showing the parts, rachilla broken above the second glume.

MELICA DIFFUSA, *Pursh.*

MELICA PORTERI Scribner.

Plant perennial.

Rootstock slender, creeping, scales distant. Roots very slender.

Culms tufted, slender, erect, 2 to 3 feet high, unbranched, glabrous.

Leaves of the stem 7 to 10; sheaths imbricated, sparingly backwardly scabrous, margins grown together; blades 6 to 12 inches long, upper sometimes shorter, 1 to 2 lines wide, flat, usually somewhat scabrous beneath, sparingly pilose above. Leaves of the root, with their sheaths, early decaying.

Inflorescence paniculate. Panicle terminal, short-pedunculate, 8 to 12 inches long; rachis terete, nearly glabrous; branches spreading in anthesis, afterwards erect, 3 inches long or less, scattered, commonly 2 at each node, one much smaller than the other. Spikelets borne singly on slender scabrous pedicels pilose and abruptly bent at the apex.

Spikelet 3- to 5-flowered, 4 to 7 lines long, slightly compressed, linear-oblong, narrowed at base and apex.

Glumes with green nerved body and broad hyaline margins and apex; first ovate, bluntly acute, 2 to 3 lines long, 1- to 5-nerved, middle nerve scabrous; second similar, one-third longer, 7-to 9-nerved; third (flowering) elliptical-oblong, narrowed to the base and apex, about 3 lines long, body rather coriaceous, scabrous on the back, with about 7 principal nerves and often with intermediate slender ones, all converging toward the apex but not uniting and not traversing the hyaline apex of the glume.

Flowers hermaphrodite. Palet oblong-lanceolate when in position, acute, ciliate on the 2 nerves, with additional inflexed membranaceous margins. Stamens 3; anthers linear, 1 line long. Stigmas cylindrical.

Grain (mature?) linear, 1 line long, dropping naked from the spikelet when ripe; pericarp rather loose, wrinkled; rachilla not disarticulating.

PLATE L; *a* and *b*, spikelet opened to show the parts. The second flower at least should have stigmas. The shorter glume in *a* is the outer one.

MELICA PORTERI, *Scrib.*

U. S. DEPARTMENT OF AGRICULTURE.

DIVISION OF BOTANY.

BULLETIN No. 12.

GRASSES OF THE SOUTHWEST.

PLATES AND DESCRIPTIONS

OF THE

GRASSES OF THE DESERT REGION OF WESTERN TEXAS, NEW MEXICO,
ARIZONA, AND SOUTHERN CALIFORNIA.

Part II.

By Dr. GEO. VASEY,

BOTANIST, DEPARTMENT OF AGRICULTURE.

ISSUED DECEMBER, 1891.

PUBLISHED BY AUTHORITY OF THE SECRETARY OF AGRICULTURE.

WASHINGTON:
GOVERNMENT PRINTING OFFICE.
1891.

NOTE.

This bulletin constitutes the second half of the first volume of a work entitled Illustrations of North American Grasses. It is designed to continue the work by a second volume to be entitled Grasses of the Pacific Coast.

LETTER OF TRANSMITTAL

WASHINGTON, *August* 3, 1891.

SIR: I have the honor of herewith presenting for publication the manuscript of the second part of the Bulletin on the "Grasses of the Southwest."

GEORGE VASEY,
Botanist.

Hon. J. M. RUSK,
Secretary of Agriculture.

INTRODUCTION.

This second part of the Grasses of the Southwest presents, like the first part,
ates and descriptions of 50 species of grasses, together making 100.

The synonymy of such as have had several names is briefly given. Most of
ie species, however, are either new, or so little known that they have received
it a single name. The drawings were made by Messrs. Scholl, Olszewski, and
olm, and in the details are generally very accurate. I wish to express my obliga-
ons to Mr. L. H. Dewey, Assistant Botanist, for important assistance in describing
ie species.

GEO. VASEY.

AUGUST 3, 1891.

5

INDEX OF PLATES.

GRASSES OF THE SOUTHWEST.

PART II.

ELIONURUS TRIPSACOIDES H. B. K. (*E. ciliaris* H. B. K.)

Plant perennial, with short rootstock, smooth throughout or with slight pubescence near the ligule.

Culms, loosely tufted, erect, branching, solid, terete, glabrous and shiny, 2 to 4 foot tall.

Leaves; radical few, the broad loose sheaths tapering into the long involute blades with scarcely a contraction at the ligule; of culm 6 to 12; sheaths rather loose, open above, lower ones exceeding internodes, upper ones shorter; blades involute, slender, 4 to 12 inches long; ligule membranaceous, ciliate, truncate, ¼ line long or less.

Inflorescence consisting of a terminal, and several distant, long-peduncled, lateral spikes. Spikes linear, 3 to 4 inches long, cylindrical; two appressed, 1-flowered spikelots at each node of the hairy rachis, one sessile and perfect, and one staminate on a stout hairy pedicel 1½ lines long.

Sessile *spikelet* narrowly lanceolate; first glume lanceolate; nearly flat, bifid at apex, acute or obtusish, rigid, herbaceous, ciliate on the prominent marginal nerves, 5 to 7 other less prominent nerves; second glume lanceolate, membranaceous, smooth, obscurely 3-nerved, 2½ to 3 lines long; third and fourth glumes lanceolate, acute, scarious, thin, smooth, the third ciliate, obscurely 3-nerved, 1½ to 2½ lines long; palet small or wanting; pedicellate spikelet similar, but all parts smaller and the first glume always acute at apex; stamens 3.

PLATE I; A, two spikelets, lower one perfect, upper one staminate, *a* to *f*, parts of perfect flower; *a*, first empty glume, extreme forms, dorsal view; and *b*, ventral view; *c*, second empty glume; *d*, third empty glume; *e*, floral glume; *f*, palet. Capital letters A, F indicate corresponding parts of staminate flower.

Dr Havard states that this grass constitutes a large portion of the vegetation of the plains of southern Texas. It occurs in Mexico, and also in Florida.

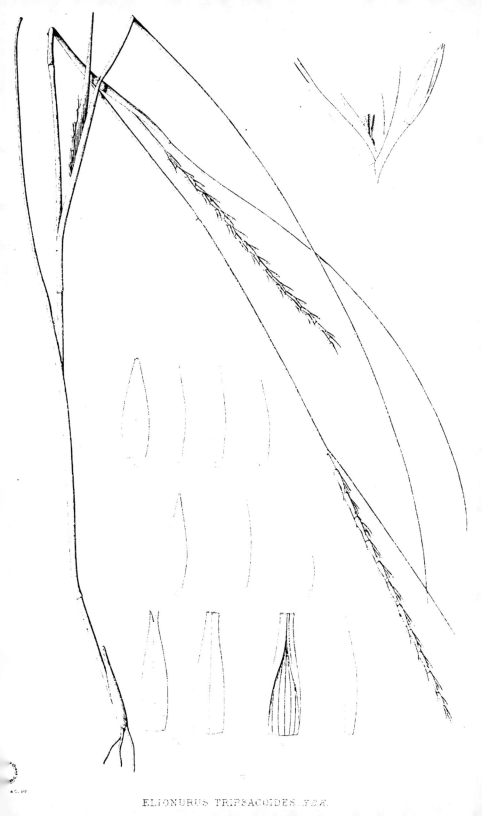

ELIONURUS TRIPSACOIDES. H.B.K.

No. 2.

HILARIA RIGIDA (Thurb.) Scrib. (*Pleuraphis rigida.* Thurb.)

Plant perennial, rigid, woody throughout, except the young growth, with hard creeping rootstock sending up scaly branches.

Culms spreading or ascending, branching freely, solid, 1 to 2 feet tall, woolly below.

Leaves of rootstock appressed, scarious scales; of culm often 2-ranked and rather crowded; sheaths longer than internodes, close, woolly; blades involute, pungent, rigid, 1 to 3 inches long; ligule a dense white, woolly collar.

Inflorescence a narrow, white or purplish spike, 2 to 3 inches long, formed of obovate clusters of 3 sessile spikelets at each node of the rachis.

Spikelets; lateral ones in the cluster staminate and 2- to 3-flowered, middle one perfect and 1-flowered; empty glumes all about 3 lines long, forming an involucre about the cluster; first glume of staminate spikelet oblong, wider above, oblique, conspicuously ciliate, 5-nerved, 1 or 2 of the nerves on one side extended in short dorsal awns, second glume obovate, 2-lobed and ciliate above, 5-to 6-nerved, with 1 or 2 dorsal awns; floral glumes oblong or wedge-shaped, nearly equally 2-lobed at apex or merely obtuse, ciliate, 3-nerved, midnerve slightly excurrent, and one lateral nerve rather obscure, 2 to 2½ lines long; palet oblong, truncate, slightly scabrous on the two nerves above, 2 lines long; empty glumes of perfect flower equal, at the back of the cluster, narrow, cuneate, oblique above, 4 to 6 awned, ciliate, 2 to 3 lines long including awns; floral glume oblong, equally 2-lobed, ciliate, 2 to 3 lines long, 3-nerved, lateral nerves equal and slightly excurrent, midnerve excurrent in an awn ¼ to 1 line long; palet lance-oblong, obtuse, ciliate or lacerate at apex, 2-nerved, 2 to 3 lines long; stigmas 2, long, plumose.

Grains; no mature grains found.

PLATE II; *a* to *d,* parts of staminate flower: *a,* first empty glume; *b,* second empty glume; *c,* floral glume; *d,* palet; *e,* perfect flower with its two empty glumes; *f* to *h,* parts of perfect flower; *f,* floral glume; *g,* palet; *h,* empty glume.

New Mexico and Arizona; almost the only grass on the driest desert land; commonly called Gayetta grass. It is considered a valuable grass.

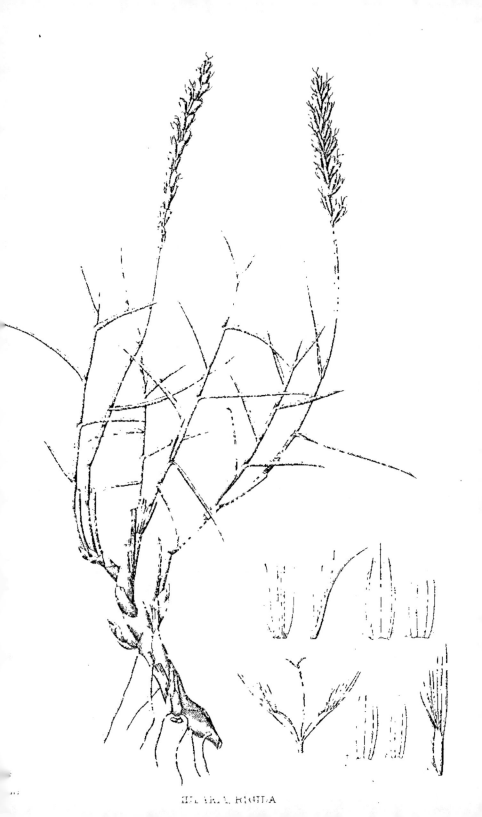

HILARIA RIGIDA

PASPALUM DISTICHUM Linn.

Plant perennial, the long creeping rootstocks rooting at the nodes and forming a rather close sod, nearly glabrous or sometimes pubescent, somewhat glaucous.

Culms one or two in a place ascending from the nodes of the rootstocks, branching, solid, angular below, 1 to 2 feet tall.

Leaves variable; of rootstocks mostly broad, loose, membranaceous scales; of culms 5 to 7; sheaths rather loose, closed, rarely compressed and open, striate; blades flat or slightly involute, 2 to 2½ lines wide, 2 to 6 inches long; ligule an inconspicuous tawny, lacerate fringe, decurrent.

Inflorescence of 2 rarely 3, narrow, erect, approximate spikes, 1 to 2½ inches long, the lower one raised on a short internode of the axis; rachis flat, bearing the two crowded rows of sessile spikelets in alternate ranks.

Spikelets broadly oblong-lanceolate, flattened, 1-flowered, 1 to 1¼ lines long; first and second glumes equal, broadly lanceolate, 3-nerved or unsymmetrically 4-nerved; first acute, 1 line long, smooth; second with short, loose pubescence; floral glume broadly lanceolate, smooth, indurated, 3-nerved, 1 line long; palet indurated, ovoid, inclosing grain, acute, obscurely 1-nerved, 1 line long and quite as broad.

Grain elliptical-lanceolate, flattened, nearly black at maturity, minutely roughened, 1 line long; falling with the enveloping palet and glume. Stigmas 2, purple, prominent.

PLATE III; *a*, first empty glume, dorsal view; *b*, second empty glume; *c*, flowering glume, inside view; *d*, palet and stamens; *e*, pistil.

Common in the Southern States, Texas, and westward to California. Near the Gulf, and in moist ground it forms valuable pasturage.

J. Holm, del.

No. 4.

PASPALUM LIVIDUM Trin.

Plant perennial, coarse, somewhat tufted on a short rootstock.

Culms few in a place, erect, or decumbent, geniculate below, solid, terete, 2 to 3 feet tall.

Leaves; radical mostly scarious; of culm 6 to 9; sheaths equaling or exceeding internode, loose, often compressed and open, lower ones often pubescent; blades flat, hispid above and below toward the tip, 3 lines wide, 2 to 6 inches long; ligule a tawny, lacerate, membranaceous fringe, ¼ line long, decurrent.

Inflorescence a racemose panicle of 4 to 8 approximate spikes, alternate on the flattened axis, 2 to 4 inches long; spikes unilateral, sessile, 1 to 1¼ inches long; rachis flat and smooth, ½ line wide, usually purplish.

Spikelets crowded, usually in 4 rows, sessile or on short pedicels, oblanceolate, flattish, 1-flowered, 1 to 1¼ lines long; first glume broadly ovate, acute, slightly convex, slightly roughened on back, 3-nerved, lateral nerves marginal and joining midnerve at apex, 1 line long; second glume same but flat and slightly smaller; floral glume, indurated, round on back, with inrolled margins, very obscurely 3-nerved, ¾ line long; palet broadly oval, indurated, nearly flat, with irregular, hyaline margins below enfolding the seed, obscurely 2-nerved, nearly 1 line long.

Grain; a careful search through 18 specimens produced but one perfect grain and that immature, but old enough to show the form, obovate, rounded, flattened on both sides ⅔ line long.

PLATE IV; *a,* first empty glume; *b,* second empty glume; *c,* floral glume, stamens, and pistil; *d,* palet, ventral view, with two membranaceous lobes turned out.

Found in southwestern Texas; common in Mexico.

No. 5.

PASPALUM PUBIFLORUM Rupt.

Plant perennial, coarse, rather glaucous.

Rootstock creeping, branching, and often rooting at the nodes.

Culms few in a place, sometimes loosely tufted, ascending or nearly erect, geniculate below, branching, solid, angular below, nearly terete above, smooth, 18 to 30 inches tall, the lower joints woolly.

Leaves of rootstocks rather coarse, loose scales; of culms 3 to 7; sheaths shorter than internodes, loose, smooth, often with a few scattered hairs along the upper margin; blade flat, 8- to 10-nerved, sparsely ciliate, 3 to 5 lines wide, 4 to 8 inches long; ligule membranaceous, ovate, lacerate, 1¼ lines long, decurrent.

Inflorescence 3 to 6 narrow, spreading spikes, alternate along the angular axis, 2 to 3 inches long; rachis flat, bearing 2, often 4, rows of crowded spikelets in alternate rows.

Spikelets broadly oblong or ovate, 1-flowered, 1 to 1¼ lines long; first glume broadly oval or hemispherical, with infolded margins, usually softly-pubescent, 3-nerved, 1¼ to 1½ lines long; second glume broadly oval, flat, with infolded margins, nearly smooth, 3-nerved, of the same length; floral glume indurate, ovate-oblong, convex, with infolded margins, smooth, obscurely 3-nerved, 1 line long; palet indurated, broadly ovate, flat, with infolded margins, smooth, obscurely 2-nerved, 1 line long.

Grain oblanceolate, thick, flat on one side, shiny, dark-brown at maturity, not translucent, 1 line long, falling free or with indurated enveloping palet.

PLATE V; *a*. spikelet, side view; *b*, first empty glume; *c*, second empty glume; *d*, floral glume; *e*, palet and stamens; *f*. pistil.

Common in Texas and extending to southern California. In the Southern States is a form with smooth spikelets. Probably a valuable pasture grass.

PHALARIS INTERMEDIA Bosc. var. ANGUSTA Chap. (*P. angusta* Nees.).

Plant perennial, rather coarse, usually glaucous throughout.

Culms somewhat tufted, erect, sometimes branching below, terete, smooth, or scabrous above, 2 to 4 feet tall.

Leaves; radical, few, 2 to 4 inches long, scarious in mature specimens; of culm 4 or 5; sheaths usually shorter than internodes, rather loose, close, smooth, blades flat, taper-pointed, scabrous on both sides, 3 to 5 lines wide, 3 to 6 inches long; ligule prominent, membranaceous, obtuse, lacerate in age, 2 to 3 lines long.

Inflorescence a dense, cylindrical spike ⅓ inch in diameter, 2 to 4 inches long; the shortly-pedicellate spikelets crowded on short, much divided, appressed branches.

Spikelets with one perfect flower, and two opposite, small rudimentary scales or glumes below the perfect flower and closely appressed against it, 1½ to 2 lines long; first and second glumes nearly equal, lanceolate, acute, carinate, slightly winged on keel above, herbaceous, hispid on keel, 1½ to 2 lines long; flowering glume coriaceous, lanceolate, acute, rounded, completely enveloping grain, clothed throughout with short, appressed, brittle hairs, nearly smooth and shining at maturity, light-brown, 1½ lines long; palet narrow, pubescent, 1 line long, 1-nerved.

Grain oval, slightly compressed, and with small hook at apex, whitish, ⅔ to 1 line long, inclosed in flowering glume from which it is extracted with difficulty.

PLATE VI; *a*, empty glumes; *b*, floral glume; *c*, palet.

Grows from Florida to Texas and California. In Texas it has been cultivated, and is a very prolific and valuable grass.

No. 7.

ARISTIDA PURPUREA Nutt.

Plant annual or short lived perennial, often purplish especially in the inflorescence.

Culms tufted, erect, slender, not branching, nearly smooth, 1 to 2 feet tall.

Leaves; radical and of radical shoots with narrow, close sheaths and slender involute blades, 4 to 10 inches long; of culm 3 or 4; lower sheaths longer than internodes, upper ones much shorter, close, smooth ; blade involute, hispid above, 3 to 6 inches long ; ligule a line of fine short hairs, somewhat hairy at the sides.

Inflorescence rather loose, narrow, erect or slightly nodding panicle, 4 to 6 inches long; branches 2 or 3 at each node, unequal, the lower 1 to 2 inches long, naked below, each bearing 2 to 5 pedicellate or nearly sessile spikelets.

Spikelets narrow, 1-flowered, 5 to 6 lines long: first glume narrowly lance-linear, emarginate, mucronate, rounded, hispid on keel, 1-nerved, 4 to $4\frac{1}{2}$ lines long: second glume same but nearly 2 lines longer; stipe hairy, $\frac{1}{4}$ line long; floral glume linear-lanceolate, rounded, slightly hispid on the nerve above, 4 lines long, terminating in 3 separate, slender, minutely hispid awns 1 to 2 inches long; palet obovate, thin, $\frac{1}{2}$ to $\frac{2}{3}$ line long.

PLATE VII; *a*, spikelet twice as large as natural size.

Abundant on plains and ridges, in several varieties, from Texas to British America. It is the earliest available grass for cattle in the spring, but of little value when mature.

D. Olszewska, del.

STIPA PENNATA Linn. var. *Neo Mexicana* Thurb.

Plant perennial with strong coarse roots.

Culms erect, densely tufted, not branching, hollow, smooth, 1 to 3 feet tall.

Leaves of radical shoots numerous, with round, close, smooth sheaths, and narrow closely involute blades, 10 to 12 inches long; of culm 3 to 4, sheaths smooth, usually exceeding internodes: blades like those of radical shoots but shorter; ligules membranaceous, rounded, and ciliate above, less than ¼ line long.

Inflorescence a narrow racemose panicle 4 to 5 inches long; branches almost appressed, the lower 2 to 3 inches long, each bearing 1 to 3 pedicellate spikelets.

Spikelets 1-flowered; first and second glumes nearly equal, lanceolate, long; awn-pointed, herbaceous, 5 to 7-nerved, 1¼ to 1½ inches long; floral glume terete, coriaceous, yellow, clothed throughout with close appressed pubescence, 5 to 7 lines long, contracted at the apex. terminating in a twisted, bent awn, feathered above, 4 to 6 inches long; palet narrowly terete, hard, smooth, 5 to 6 lines long.

Grain narrow, reddish, 2 to 3 lines long.

PLATE VIII; *a*, spikelet dissected. about natural size.

Texas, New Mexico, and Arizona.

No. 9.

STIPA SCRIBNERI Vasey.

Rootstock short, horizontal, with coarse fibrous roots.

Culms tufted, erect, terete, smooth, 1½ to 2¼ feet tall, unbranched.

Leaves; from base half as long as the culm; of stem 3 or 4; sheaths smooth, or lower ones slightly scabrous, nearly equaling or slightly exceeding the internodes, close; blade flat below, involute above toward the long tapering point, midnerve inconspicuous, 1 to 2 lines wide, 4 to 10 inches long; ligule truncate, 1 line long.

Inflorescence an erect slender panicle, its base inclosed by the upper sheath, narrow and close, 5 to 8 inches long; rachis slightly angular, not flexuous; branches in twos or threes, appressed, 1 to 2 inches long, each bearing 2 to 4 spikelets on short pedicels.

Spikelets 1-flowered; empty glumes unequal, the first 6 to 7 lines, and second 5 lines long, linear-lanceolate, acuminate, both 3-nerved, smooth; floral glume about 4 lines long, white-hairy, the hairs longer above forming a crown or tuft 1 line long; awn rather slender, 8 to 9 lines long, not hairy; stipe short, acute; palet less than 1 line long, obtuse, and adherent to grain.

Grain nearly cylindrical, yellow, opaque, 2 to 2¼ lines long.

PLATE IX; *a*, spikelet dissected and enlarged.

Arizona and New Mexico. Generally in strong tufts.

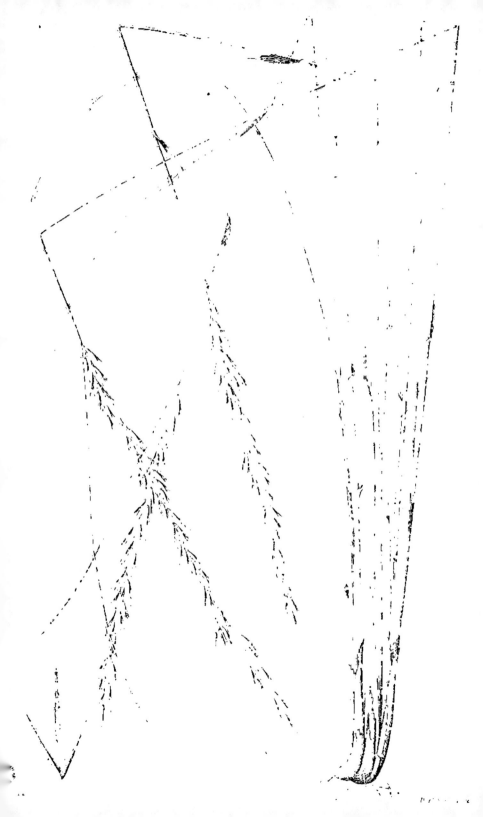

No. 10.

ORYZOPSIS MEMBRANACEA (Pursh.). (*Stipa membranacea* Pursh.)
Eriocoma cuspidata Nutt.)

Plant perennial, closely tufted, thickened at base.

Culms slender, nearly erect, not branching, geniculate, solid, terete, smooth, 12 to 18 inches tall.

Leaves; radical, numerous, the scarious sheaths clustered thick about the base of the culms; blades involute, smooth, 6 to 10 inches long; of the culms 3; lower sheaths shorter than internodes, smooth and close, upper sheath longer and loose; blades like those of radical leaves; ligule membranaceous, ovate, acute, or lacerate, 1 line long, prominently decurrent.

Inflorescence a very loose, erect or flexuous panicle 4 to 6 inches long, included at the base, usually with 2 or 3 nearly equal axes; branches mostly in pairs, distant, horizontal, divided in pairs beyond the middle, bearing solitary spikelets on long flexuous pedicels.

Spikelets 1-flowered, 3 lines long; first and second glumes equal, inflated and widened below, narrowed above to a long sharp point, scarious except the 5 rather obscure nerves, minutely pubescent throughout, 3 lines long; floral glume ovoid or oblong, hard, dark-brown, profusely clothed with long white hairs, 1½ lines long, obscurely nerved, terminating in an awn 2 lines long, which falls at maturity; palet conical, smooth, hard, brown, obscurely nerved, 1½ lines long.

Grain oval, light-yellow, ⅔ line long.

PLATE X; *a*, spikelet; *b*, empty glumes; *c*, floral glume, with hairs and awn; *d*, same after hairs and awn have fallen; *e*, palet. In the floral glume, *c*, the awn should be represented more to one side.

Texas to California, northward to British Columbia, usually in sandy or gravelly soil. A valuable grass. The large seeds are nutritious, and cattle fatten where the grass is abundant.

ORYZOPSIS FIMBRIATA Hemsl. (*Stipa fimbriata* Kth.)

Culms tufted with many root leaves at base, erect, striate, smooth, slender, 1 to 2 feet tall.

Leaves of stem 2 to 4; lower sheaths much shorter than internodes, closely wrapping the culm with the membranaceous inner fold; blade filiform, involute. ¼ line wide, 1 to 3 inches long, much exceeded by the involute setaceous root leaves; ligule conspicuous, obtuse, wider than blade, 1 line long.

Inflorescence a loose, erect, or spreading panicle, 4 to 6 inches long; rachis angular, slightly scabrous, flexuous toward apex, branches in twos or threes, spreading or lower ones even deflexed, filiform, 1 to 2 inches long, each bearing 2 to 4 spikelets on pedicels 3 to 5 lines long.

Spikelets obovate, 2 to 2½ lines long; first glume broadly lanceolate, upper half scarious with acuminate apex, often purplish, 5-nerved, smooth, 2 to 2½ lines long; second glume same but slightly smaller; floral glume coriaceous, orbicular, obscurely 5-nerved, covered with loose white hairs longer at base, and bearing a smooth flexuous awn 5 to 8 lines long; palet obovate, acuminate, 2-nerved, 1¼ lines long.

PLATE XI; *a*, spikelet dissected and enlarged; *b*, panicle at maturity.

Texas, New Mexico, and Arizona.

W H Scholl del

MUHLENBERGIA BUCKLEYANA Scribn. (*Muhlenbergia Texana* Buckl. not *Thurb.*)

Plant annual, diffuse, spreading.

Culms tufted at base, spreading, terete, slender, smooth, branching below, 10 to 15 inches tall.

Radical leaves few and small; of culm 1 to 3, usually 2; sheaths rather loose, somewhat vaginate, or compressed and open, slightly scabrous, longer than internodes; blade flat or involute, scabrous on both sides, 1 to 2 inches long.

Inflorescence an oblong, loose, spreading panicle 4 to 8 inches long; rachis and branches slender, terete, often purple, the latter mostly alternate, 1 to 3 inches long, bearing solitary spikelets on slender pedicels 1 to 2 lines long.

Spikelets narrowly lanceolate, 1-flowered, 1 line long; first glume ovate, acute, hyaline, pubescent, 1-nerved, $\frac{1}{4}$ line long with a very short awn; second glume same but little larger; floral glume oblong, 2-toothed at apex, $\frac{1}{2}$ to 1 line long, 3-nerved, slightly pubescent on the nerves, midnerve excurrent in an awn as long as the glume; palet lanceolate, nearly acute, thin, 2-nerved, $\frac{1}{2}$ line long.

Grain narrowly obovate, rounded at apex, compressed, reddish-amber, $\frac{1}{4}$ line long, falling with floral glume and palet but easily escaping.

PLATE XII; *a*, spikelet enlarged; *b*, empty glumes; *c*, floral glume; *d*, palet.

Texas, New Mexico to Mexico on rocky hills.

No. 13.

MUHLENBERGIA NEO-MEXICANA Vasey.

Plant slender, tufted, perennial, from thick, knotted, or sometimes creeping rootstocks.

Culm branching freely below, erect, slender, terete, nearly smooth, 12 to 18 inches tall.

Leaves ; of culms 4 to 6; sheaths longer than internodes, close, slightly roughened; blades erect, appressed, closely involute and setaceous, 2 to 3 inches long; ligule an irregular, ovate, lacerate membrane ¼ line long.

Inflorescence a narrow, erect or slightly nodding panicle, 3 to 4 inches long, often purple; branches alternate, erect, hispid, ½ to 1 inch long, bearing rather close clusters of spikelets on hispid pedicels ¼ to 1½ lines long.

Spikelets narrow, 1-flowered, 2 lines long; empty glumes equal, lance-ovate, acute, carinate, hyaline, 1-nerved, 1 line long, terminating in a slender awn ¼ to ½ line long; floral glume narrowly conical, lanceolate, acute when unrolled, thin, smooth, minutely pubescent at base, 3-nerved, terminating in an awn ½ inch long; palet obscurely 2-nerved, 2 lines long, often projecting out of the floral glume; stamens 3.

Grain, none present in the 24 specimens examined.

PLATE XIII ; *a*, panicle at maturity; *b*, cluster of spikelets; *c*, spikelet enlarged.

Rocky ledges, New Mexico and Arizona.

No. 14.

MUHLENBERGIA SCHAFFNERI Fourn.

Plant low, annual or short-lived perennial.

Culms tufted, procumbent or spreading, branching freely, 2 to 4 inches tall.

Leaves; radical, few and small; of culm 3 to 5; sheaths compressed, open, striate, scabrous on both sides, margins white, ½ to 1 inch long; ligule membranaceous, lacerate, ⅔ line long, decurrent in prominent hyaline margins on the sheath.

Inflorescence a narrow contracted panicle, 1 to 2 inches long, often included at base, rachis and branches angular, hispid.

Spikelets sessile, appressed, narrow, 1½ to 2 lines long; first glume lanceolate, the apex lobed, with 2 short unequal or nearly equal teeth at apex, hispid, 2-nerved, herbaceous, rigid, 1 to 1¼ lines long; second glume linear-lanceolate, acute, carinate, short-awned at apex, hispid, 1-nerved, 1½ to 2¼ lines long, including awn; floral glume ovate, 2 minute hyaline teeth at apex, slightly hispid, ciliate below, 3-nerved, with slender awn ¾ to 2 lines long, or sometimes awnless; palet ovate, acute, 2-nerved, thin, smooth, 1¼ to 1½ lines long.

Grain narrowly cylindrical, reddish amber color, ¾ line long, falling with palet and glume but easily escaping.

PLATE XIV, No. 2, lower figure; *a*, first empty glume; *b*, second empty glume; *c*, floral glume; *d*, palet.

Arizona.

No. 14.

MUHLENBERGIA DEPAUPERATA Scrib.

Plant low, tufted, annual or short lived perennial.

Culms spreading, branching at each node, 3 to 4 inches tall.

Leaves; radical, few or none; of culm 2 to 4, with loose, smooth, broad, open sheaths, and short folded or involute blades; ligule membranaceous, lacerate, decurrent.

Inflorescence a narrow, contracted, rather close panicle, 2 to 3 inches long, usually included below, rachis and branches angular, hispid, pedicels short.

Spikelets narrow, 1-flowered, 1½ to 2 lines long; first glume ovate, obliquely 2-toothed at apex, scarious, minutely hispid, obscurely 1-nerved, ¾ to 1 line long; second glume lanceolate, narrowing at apex to a slender, awn-like point, scarious, minutely hispid, 1 to 1¼ lines long; floral glume narrowly lanceolate, with 2 minute teeth at apex, rounded on back, hispid, 3-nerved, 1½ to 2 lines long, midnerve excurrent in an awn 2 to 5 lines long; palet lanceolate, acuminate, rounded, enveloping grain, minutely pubescent, 2-nerved, 1¼ to 1¾ lines long.

Grain narrowly cylindrical, reddish-amber, lighter above, 1 line long, falling with palet and glume but easily escaping.

PLATE XIV, No. 1, upper figure; *a*, spikelet enlarged; *b*, empty glumes; *c*, floral glume; *d*, palet.

Very close to *M. Schaffneri* and perhaps but a variety of it.

Arizona.

No. 15.

LYCURUS PHLEOIDES H. B. K.

Plant perennial from thickened, slightly bulbous base.

Culms tufted, erect or ascending, rather weak, branching, solid, nearly terete, smooth, 1 to 2 feet tall.

Leaves; radical numerous, with short, close sheaths and flat, folded or involute blades 1 to 2 inches long, with white margins and midrib: of culm 4 or 5; sheaths much shorter than internodes, loose and open, smooth; blades like those of radical leaves but longer; ligule membranaceous, ovate, acute, oblique, decurrent on one side, 1 line long.

Inflorescence a dense, cylindrical spike ¼ inch in diameter, 2 to 3 inches long.

Spikelets 1 to 3 on each of the short branches of the rachis, one or two of which are commonly imperfect; first glume oblong, thin, 2-nerved, ½ to ¾ line long, terminating in 2 or (rarely) 3, unequal, hispid awns, 1 to 3 lines long; second glume ovate, acute, carinate, membranaceous, 1-nerved, ¾ to 1 line long, terminating in an awn 2 to 3 lines long; floral glume lanceolate-oblong, acute, pubescent throughout, thicker than the empty glumes, 3-nerved, 1¼ to 2 lines long, terminating in a hispid awn 1½ to 2 lines long; palet lanceolate, 2-toothed at apex, rounded, 2-nerved, thinly pubescent, 1¼ lines long; the flowers are subject to the attack of an insect, which renders the palet inflated and hardened below.

Grain narrowly lanceolate or linear, yellow, ¼ line long.

PLATE XV; A, perfect spikelet, with abortive spikelet below; *a*, spikelet with the palet distorted; *b*, first empty glume; *c*, second empty glume; *d*, floral glume, ventral view; *e*, palet; *f*, palet of pistillate flower distorted by an insect.

Texas and Mexico, northward to Colorado.

SPOROBOLUS ARGUTUS Kth. (*Vilfa Arkansana* Trin. *Vilfa arguta* Nees.)

Plant annual, smooth throughout except the scabrous margins of the leaves. *Culm* tufted, spreading, weak, branching below, smooth, 6 to 12 inches tall.

Leaves of radical shoots numerous, with mostly smooth, loose, scarious sheaths and flat blades 2 to 3 inches long; of culm 2 or 3, lower sheaths mostly shorter than internodes, close; blades like those of radical shoots, but upper ones much shorter; ligule a line of short tawny bristles.

Inflorescence a rather narrow or sometimes spreading, erect panicle, 2 to 3 inches long, often included at base; branches 3 to 5 at base, alternate above, divided and bearing many pedicellate spikelets on the outer two-thirds.

Spikelets oblong-ovate, 1-flowered, ¾ line long; first glume oblong, obtusish, thin, hyaline, smooth, 1-nerved, ½ line long; floral glume lance-ovate, acute, thin, 1-nerved, ⅔ line long; palet broadly ovate, thin, obscurely 2-nerved, ⅔ line long.

Grain elliptical, compressed, light-brown, with reddish scar, utricular, falling free.

PLATE XVI; *a*, empty glumes enlarged; *b*, floral glume and palet inclosing grain.

Texas to Arizona and Mexico.

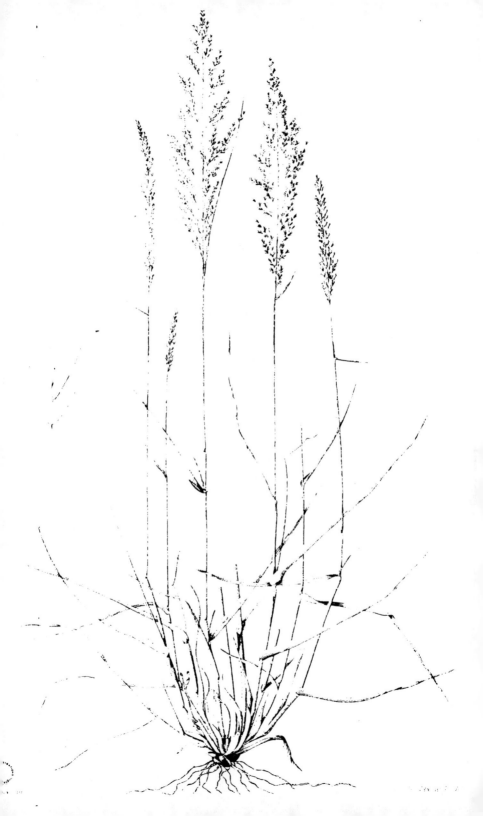

SPOROBOLUS BUCKLEYI Vasey.

Culms erect, loosely tufted, slender, not branching. compressed, especially below, smooth, 2 to 3 feet tall.

Leaves; radical, few, sheaths green or purplish, compressed, tapering into slender, mostly folded, smooth, long pointed blades, 6 to 15 inches long, green at maturity; of culm 4 or 5; sheaths mostly exceeding internodes, lower ones compressed and open, upper close, blades like those of radical leaves; ligule a minute tawny fringe.

Inflorescence a loose, spreading, erect panicle, 10 to 15 inches long; branches spreading or becoming reflexed, mostly alternate, 3 to 5 inches long, slender, bearing beyond the lower third, short branches of pedicellate spikelets.

Spikelets obovate, 1-flowered, ⅔ line long; first glume lanceolate, acute, thin, smooth, 1-nerved, ¼ line long: second glume same. but nearly twice as large; floral glume ovate, acuminate. hyaline, smooth. 1-nerved, ⅔ line long; palet lance-ovate, acute, obscurely 2-keeled, ½ line long, in age splitting to the base.

Grain elliptical-globose, utricle light-brown, ¼ line long.

PLATE XVII; *a,* spikelet enlarged.

Well distinguished by the large panicle of capillary branches and many flowered, small spikelets. A handsome species.

Texas to Mexico.

No. 18.

SPOROBOLUS INTERRUPTUS Vasey. (*Vilfa interrupta* Vasey in Special Report No. 63, Department of Agriculture, 1883.)

Plant perennial, with densely tufted, bulbous base.

Culms erect, not branching, smooth, terete, 1 to 2 foot tall.

Leaves; radical and from radical shoots, numerous, with scarious, often reddish, glabrous or pubescent, tapering sheaths, and mostly flat, smooth or loosely pubescent erect blades, 3 to 5 inches long; of culm 2 or 3; sheaths longer than internodes, close, open above, smooth blades, mostly involute, erect, 1 line wide, 1 to 3 inches long; ligule a narrow ciliate fringe.

Inflorescence a narrow, open or interrupted, erect panicle, 4 to 6 inches long; rachis flexuous, branches alternate or verticillate below, in twos or threes above, 1 to 2 inches long.

Spikelets short-pedicellate, narrow, 1- or 2-flowered, 2 to 3 lines long; first glume lanceolate, acute, carinate, scarious, smooth, 1-nerved, 1 to 1¼ lines long; second glume ovate-lanceolate, nearly twice as large; floral glume ovate-lanceolate, acute, membranaceous, smooth, 1-nerved or obscurely 3-nerved above, 2 to 3 lines long; palet broadly lanceolate, bifid at apex, thin, hyaline, smooth, slightly 2-keeled, 2 lines long; anthers 3, long, reddish purple; stigmas 2, greenish, plumose.

Grain, no mature grains seen.

PLATE XVIII; *a*, spikelet enlarged; *b*, empty glumes; *c*, floral glume; *d*, palet; 2, typical panicle.

Arizona.

No. 19.

SPOROBOLUS TRICHOLEPIS (Torr). (*Vilfa tricholepis* Torr.)

Plant slender, perennial, often purplish in culm and inflorescence, smooth throughout.

Culms tufted, erect, seldom branching, smooth, slightly compressed, 1 to 2 feet tall.

Leaves of radical shoots with rather loose, scarious sheaths and narrow involute blades 2 to 4 inches long; of culm 2 or 3; sheaths close, nearly equaling or exceeding internodes, blades involute, erect, 2 to 3 inches long; ligule membranaceous, truncate, lacerate, decurrent, ¼ line long or less.

Inflorescence an ovate, pyramidal, erect, or flexuous panicle, 4 to 6 inches long; branches mostly alternate, slightly spreading, 1 to 2 inches long, divided and rather loosely flowered on the upper two-thirds.

Spikelets on long slender pedicels, lanceolate, 1-flowered, 1½ lines long; first and second glumes nearly equal lanceolate, acute or obtuse, carinate, thin, smooth, 1-nerved, 1 to 1¼ lines long; floral glume lanceolate, acute, or obtuse, membranaceous, pubescent or villous on the 3 nerves, 1¼ lines long; palet lanceolate, acute, membranaceous, slightly ciliate above, pubescent on the 2 approximate nerves, or nearly smooth, 1½ lines long.

Grain narrowly elliptical, compressed, yellow, ½ line long.

PLATE XIX; *a*, empty glumes; *b*, floral glume and palet opened to show stamens and pistil.

Mexico northward to Colorado.

No. 20.

SPOROBOLUS WRIGHTII Munro in Herb.

Plant perennial, coarse, with thickened bulbous base.
Culms erect, not branching, terete, smooth and shining, 2 to 4 feet tall.

Leaves; radical, few, scarious sheaths at maturity; of culm 4 or 5; sheaths mostly exceeding internodes, closed, slightly hairy at the throat; blades flat or involute, 2 or 3 lines wide, 1 to 2 feet long; ligule a minute fringe.

Inflorescence a slender, erect, lanceolate panicle, 10 to 13 inches long; branches mostly alternate, slender, erect-spreading, 1 to 4 inches long, bearing many shortly-pedicellate spikelets on the outer two-thirds.

Spikelets lanceolate, 1-flowered, 1 line long; first glume ovate, barely acute, membranaceous, 1-nerved, ¼ to ½ line long; second glume same, but twice as large; floral glume broadly lanceolate, acute, membranaceous, smooth, 1-nerved, ¾ line long; palet lanceolate, cleft at apex, slightly 2-keeled, ⅔ line long.

Grain elliptical, compressed, brown, ⅓ line long.

PLATE XX; *a*, spikelet enlarged.

A tall coarse grass, growing in dense tufts, commonly called Saccaton or Zacate. Probably too coarse to be of agricultural value.

Western Texas to southern California.

No. 21.

TRISETUM HÁLLII Scrib.

Plant annual.

Culms slender, not branching, geniculate, ascending, scabrous. 1 to 1¼ feet tall.

Leaves; radical, few and small; of culm 3 or 4; sheaths usually exceeding internodes, open above, somewhat scabrous; blades flat or slightly involute, taper-pointed, scabrous on both sides, 1 to 1½ lines wide, 3 to 5 inches long; ligule membranaceous, truncate, lacerate, 1 line long.

Inflorescence a rather narrow, contracted, close, erect, or flexuous panicle, 4 to 6 inches long, included or but slightly exserted; branches mostly in threes, slightly spreading, ¼ to 1 inch long, bearing pedicellate spikelets; crowded along their entire length.

Spikelets obovate, 3- to 4-flowered, upper one sterile, small and abortive, 2 to 2½ lines long; first glume narrowly lanceolate, acute, herbaceous, hispid on keel, 3-nerved, ¼ line wide, 2 lines long; second glume oblong-lanceolate, 5-nerved, twice as wide as the first; internode of rachilla slender, curved, articulate above, smooth, ¼ line long; floral glume lanceolate, with two attenuate teeth at apex, scarious, scabrid, 1½ to 2 lines long, obscurely 3-nerved, mid-nerve excurrent in a slender awn 2 to 4 lines long; palet narrowly linear, lanceolate when spread out, thin, 2-keeled, 1 line long, not inclosed in floral glume.

Grains, none found in the specimens examined

PLATE XXI; *a*, spikelet; *b*, empty glumes; *c*, floral glume; *d*, palet.

This differs from *T. interruptum* Buckl. in its heavier panicle, shorter teeth of the flowering glume, and the higher insertion of the awn. Both species occur in Texas.

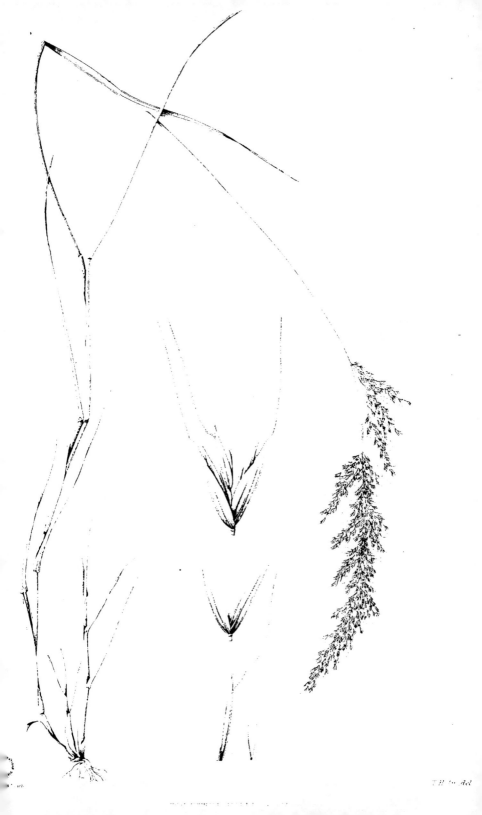

No. 22.

TRISETUM INTERRUPTUM Buckley.

Plant slender, tufted, annual, rather glaucous throughout.
Roots numerous, fine.
Culms ascending, geniculate, branching, terete. smooth. 6 to 18 inches tall.

Leaves of radical shoots numerous, with smooth or cinerous-pubescent sheaths and flat blades, hispid above, 2 to 3 inches long; of culm 3 to 5; sheaths usually little shorter than internodes. smooth or somewhat scabrous or pubescent; blades flat or involute, scabrous, 2 to 3 inches long; ligule membranaceous, lacerate. obliquely truncate, 1 line long.

Inflorescence a narrow, somewhat interrupted, erect or flexuous panicle, 3 to 5 inches long; branches in 2's or 3's of unequal length, ½ to 1 inch long.

Spikelets sessile, obovate, 3- to 4-flowered, upper one sterile or small and abortive, 2 to 2½ lines long; first glume oblanceolate, acute, herbaceous. hispid on keel, 3-nerved, 1½ to 2 lines long; second glume same, but twice as wide and 5-nerved; internode of rachilla curved, glabrous, ½ line long; floral glume lanceolate, rounded on back, scarious above, rigid, smooth, about 2 lines long, 3-nerved, ending in 2 slender teeth, 2 lateral nerves uniting above with the midnerve and forming above the middle a slender hispid awn, 2 to 3 lines long; palet narrowly linear, wider at top, lanceolate when spread out, thin, smooth, 2-keeled, cleft at apex, standing out of floral glume, 1 line long.

Grain yellowish, opaque, elliptical, flattened, 1 line long.

PLATE XXII; *a*, floral glume, side view; *b*, palet; *c*, spikelet; *d* (marked *a* in plate), empty glumes. The floral glume, *a*, is not well figured.

Abundant in Texas.

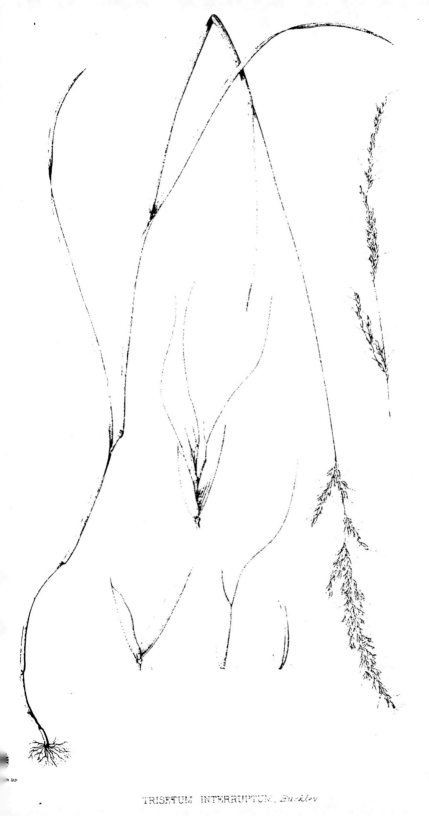

TRISETUM INTERRUPTUM, Buckley

CHLORIS SWARTZIANA Döll. (*Chloris petræa* Swz. non. Thunb.)
(*Schultesia petræa* Spreng.) (? *Eustachys petræa* Desv.)

Plant perennial, from short rootstock, light green or more or less purplish throughout.

Culm erect, or geniculate and spreading below, frequently branched, flatly compressed, smooth, 1 to 2 feet tall.

Leaves; radical, with closely compressed, smooth, equitant, divergent sheaths, and flat or folded blades, round-pointed, scabrous on the edge, 2 lines wide, 4 to 10 inches long; of stem 3 to 5, sometimes opposite; sheaths compressed, loose, smooth, shorter than internodes; lower blades like those of radical leaves but shorter, and upper ones reduced to nearly none; ligule a minute, ciliate, membranaceous fringe.

Inflorescence a digitate cluster of 3 to 6 sessile, linear, erect, slightly spreading spikes, 2 to 3 inches long, bearing the crowded sessile spikelets in two rows on one side of the slender, scabrid rachis.

Spikelets 2-flowered, upper flower sterile; first glume broadly ovate-acute, smooth, 1-nerved, scarious, ½ line long; second glume obovate, 2 minutely toothed lobes at apex and a short hispid awn formed by the excurrent nerve, hispid on back, ¾ to 1 line long; floral glume, rotund, broadly acute, or rounded and mucronate, coriaceous, brown, ciliate, pubescent on the lower two-thirds of the single nerve, smooth above; palet ovate-lanceolate, convex, obscurely 2-nerved, 1 line long; sterile flower a broadly ovate, truncate glume, folded triangular, brown, ¼ line long.

Grain translucent, creamy-white, triangular, ½ line long, falling with spikelet intact except the empty glumes which are left on the rachis.

PLATE XXIII; *a*, spikelet; *b*, floral glume, sterile flower, stamens and stigmas; *c*, second empty glume; *d*, first empty glume; palet not shown.

Low grounds near the Gulf, from Florida westward to Texas.

No. 24.

TRICHLORIS PLURFLORA Fourn.

Plant rather coarse, somewhat glaucous throughout or purplish in the inflorescence.

Culms few, from loosely tufted, slightly bulbous base, erect, solid, terete, smooth, rarely branching, 2 to 3 feet tall.

Leaves; radical and from sterile culms, numerous, with loose sheaths, and flat, taper-pointed blades, 3 to 4 lines wide and 8 to 10 inches long, scabrous above and below, with scattered hairs. near the ligule; of stem 5 to 7; sheath equaling or exceeding internode, loose and open above, smooth; blade like that of the radical leaves; ligule a row of rusty, fine hairs ¼ line long.

Inflorescence an obovate panicle of 10 to 15 slightly spreading, narrow, sessile approximate spikes, scattered one or two in a place along the short rachis. Spikes unilateral, rachis hispid, 2 to 4 inches long.

Spikelets nearly sessile, with 3 or 4 flowers. the upper ones sterile; first glume narrowly-lanceolate, terminating in an awn-like point, hyaline, about 1 line long; second glume larger, 1½ to 2 lines long; floral glumes narrowly-lanceolate, scabrous, ciliate on the margins, 1-nerved, 2 lines long, terminating in 3 hispid awns, middle one 4 lines and lateral ones about 1 line long; palet lanceolate, acute, 2-nerved, hyaline margins infolded; upper sterile glumes same as floral glumes but smaller and lateral awns sometimes minute.

Grain yellow, narrowly triangular, ⅓ line long.

PLATE XXIV; *a*, spikelet; *b*, floral glume; *c*, palet; *d*, empty glumes.

Texas to Mexico.

TRICHLORIS VERTICILLATA Fourn. (*Chloropsis Blanchardiana* Gay in Herb.*)

Plant perennial, mostly glaucous, or light-green, or purplish in the inflorescence. *Culms* tufted from somewhat bulbous base, erect or sometimes prostrate below and rooting at the lower nodes, terete, solid, smooth, 1 to 2½ feet tall.

Leaves; radical and from sterile culms, with compressed, hairy-fringed sheaths and hispid, flat or somewhat revolute, slender-pointed blades 3 to 8 inches long; of stem usually 4; lower sheaths equaling nodes, upper ones often much shorter, striate, hispid, hairy along the margins, blade flat or V-shaped with revolute margins, hispid above and below and with scattered white hairs above the ligule, which is a dense row of fine white hairs ¼ line long.

Inflorescence an umbellate cluster of 8 to 12 or more narrow, sessile, slightly spreading spikes, 3 to 4 inches long, with the spikelets narrowly-sessile in two rows on one side of the hispid rachis.

Spikelets lance-linear, with one fertile and one sterile flower: first glume linear-lanceolate, acute or short awned, hyaline, 1-nerved, ⅓ to ¼ line long; second glume ovate, ¾ line long, with an awn of equal length; third or floral glume narrowly lanceolate, scabrous on back, obscurely 3-nerved, 1¼ lines long, terminating in 3 scabrous awns 5 to 9 lines long; palet lance-linear, ciliate at the rounded apex, hyaline, 2-nerved, 1¼ lines long; fourth (sterile) glume, cylindrical, filiform, 1 line long, terminating in 3 hispid awns 3 to 6 lines long.

Grain lance-elliptic, triangular in cross section, translucent, light yellow, with light orange chit, falling with the spikelet, entire except the persistent empty glumes.

PLATE XXV; *a,* and *b,* spikelets enlarged.

Texas, Arizona to Mexico.

No. 26.

SCHEDONNARDUS TEXANUS Steud. (*Lepturus paniculatus* Nutt.)

Plant a low straggling annual.

Culm tufted and branching at base, spreading, slender, terete, or compressed, hollow, minutely pubescent.

Leaves: radical and from radical shoots, numerous, folded, spirally twisted, with short, cartilaginous points; of culm 1 or 2 equaled or exceeded by those of the base; sheaths loose, compressed, open above; blades flat or folded, spirally twisted, smooth, 2 to 3 inches long; ligule ovate, acute, lacerate, decurrent in scarious margins down the sheath.

Inflorescence a loose racemose panicle, the spikelets sessile and appressed in excavations in the horizontally spreading branches, which are 1 to 4 inches long, alternate and distant on the triangular hispid rachis.

Spikelets 1-flowered, narrow, 1½ to 2 lines long; first glume lanceolate, sometimes toothed on the margin, scarious-margined, ¾ line long, sometimes 1 sided, 1 prominent hispid nerve, sometimes excurrent in an awn one-half as long as the glume; second glume same but nearly twice as large; floral glume narrowly lanceolate, acute or mucronulate, 3-nerved, rounded on back, hispid on the midnerve, slightly pubescent at base, 1½ lines long; palet ovate, obtuse, or slightly toothed, round on back, hyaline, 2-nerved, 1¼ to 1½ lines long.

Grain dark reddish, translucent-amber, with darker oblique chit extending one-third way from base, narrowly cylindrical, 1 line long, falling free or with disarticulate branch.

PLATE XXVI; *a*, branch with spikelets in position; *b*, spikelet; *c*, second empty glume; *d*, first empty glume; *e*, palet; *f*, floral glume.

Texas to Arizona, northward to Dakota and British America.

T. Heir. a.

No. 27.

PAPPOPHORUM APERTUM Munro, in Herb.

Plant perennial, loosely tufted with somewhat bulbous base.

Culms erect, not branched, solid, terete, smooth, 18 to 30 inches tall.

Leaves; radical few and small; from radical shoots, with slightly hispid sheaths, and narrow, involute blades, 4 to 10 inches long; of culm 3 or 4; sheaths nearly equaling or often exceeding internodes, slightly hispid; blade involute, hispid above, 2 lines wide with long tapering point, 6 to 10 inches long; ligule a rather conspicuous, loose hairy fringe 1½ to 2 lines long.

Inflorescence a close, linear, spike-like, panicle, 6 to 10 inches long, with short branches below, none above, often included at base.

Spikelets oblong, 3-flowered (upper one sterile), 2 lines long, on short hispid pedicels less than ½ line long; first glume lanceolate acute, carinate, hyaline, minutely hispid on keel, 1-nerved, 1¾ lines long; second glume same but ¼ line longer; floral glumes vasiform, nearly square unrolled, pubescent especially below, 1 line long, 7-nerved, each nerve terminating in a hispid awn 2 lines long, and alternating with these are 7 or 8 slightly smaller awns; sterile glume similar but half as large and raised on an internode of the rachilla ½ line long; palet lanceolate, lacerate at apex, 2-keeled, 1½ lines long.

Grain narrowly lanceolate, light brown, 1 line long, falling with the entire spikelet, except the persistent empty glumes.

PLATE XXVII; *a,* spikelet; *b,* empty glumes; *c,* floral glume; *d,* palet; *e,* sterile upper flower

There is a variety of this species with much looser inflorescence, the lower branches 1 to 2 inches long, flowering mostly to the base and subdivided; spikelets purplish.

Western Texas to Arizona.

PAPPOPHORUM WRIGHTII Watson. (*P. boreale* Torr. non Griseb.)

Plant perennial (?) from densely tufted, bulbous base.

Roots fibrous, flexuous.

Culms erect or ascending, geniculate at the lower nodes, branching, slender, solid, terete, minutely pubescent with long white hairs at the nodes, 10 to 15 inches tall.

Leaves of radical shoots numerous, minutely pubescent, blade filiform-involute, 2 to 4 inches long; of culm 4 to 6; sheaths shorter than the internodes, loose, open; blade filiform-involute, 1 to 3 inches long; ligule a dense line of hairs ¼ inch long.

Inflorescence a compact, spike-like panicle, 1 to 3 inches long, simple, or with numerous short appressed branches below.

Spikelets on short hispid pedicels, about 3-flowered, 1 line long; empty glumes lanceolate, acutish, 5-nerved; hyaline, sparsely pubescent, ¾ line long; second glume same but ¼ longer; floral glumes broadly oval, pubescent, 1 line long and nearly as broad; 5 nerves terminating in feathered awns 1¼ lines long, purple at base, 4 similar intermediate awns alternating; sterile glume similar but smaller and raised on a longer internode of the rachilla; palet elliptical, hyaline, 2-keeled, nerves rather inconspicuous, ¾ line long.

Grain about oval, dull-yellow, falling with the floret.

PLATE XXVIII; *a*, spikelet dissected; *b*, sterile flowers; *c*, floral glume; *d*, palet.

Texas to California and Mexico.

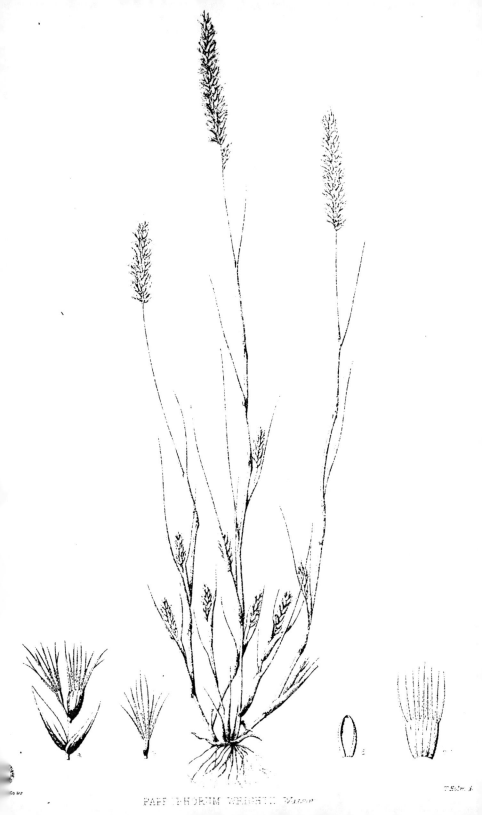

PASPALORUM WRIGHTII *Vasey*

COTTEA PAPPOPHOROIDES Kunth.

Plant perennial from a short, scaly rootstock, light green or often purplish in the inflorescence and lower sheaths.

Culms loosely tufted at base, erect or somewhat spreading, branching, hollow, terete, pubescent, 1 to 2 feet tall.

Leaves; radical and from radical shoots few and small; of culm 7 to 10, sheaths close, minutely cinerous pubescent, nearly equaling or usually exceeding the internodes; blade flat or involute toward the tapering point, somewhat scabrous on both sides, 1½ to 2 lines wide, 3 to 6 inches long; ligule a minute hairy fringe.

Inflorescence a rather close, or becoming loose, lanceolate or narrowly pyramidal panicle, 3 to 6 inches long, peduncle but little exserted, rachis pubescent, nearly terete; branches mostly alternate, flower-bearing nearly to the base, slightly spreading, 1 to 2 inches long, bearing the spikelets on short pubescent pedicels.

Spikelets obovate, flat, 7- to 10-flowered, 3 to 4 lines long; empty glumes oblong or oblong-ovate, nearly equal, 2 lines long; first glume irregularly 3-toothed at apex, about 13-nerved, pubescent on back, margins hyaline; second glume acutish or short awned, about 9-nerved, with hyaline margins, less pubescent than first glume; floral glumes obovate, 1 to 1½ lines long, pubescent especially at base, about 15-nerved, cleft above into 11 narrow divisions, the outer more deeply cleft, and ciliate on the margins, with long white hairs, each terminating in a hispid awn ½ to 1½ lines long; palet lanceolate, with 2 pubescent nerves continuing and connivent about the cleft apex, narrow hyaline margins infolded, 1½ lines long.

Grain, dull whitish yellow, oblong, slightly curved, falling with the disarticulated spikelet or easily escaping free.

PLATE XXIX; *a*, spikelet; *b*, empty glumes; *c*, floral glumes; *c'*, part of apex of floral glume enlarged; *d*, palet; *d'*, apex of palet. The figure *b* does not show the full number of nerves.

Texas to Arizona and Mexico.

No. 30.

SCLEROPOGON KARWINSKIANUS Benth. (*Lesourdia* Fourn.)

Plant perennial, from horizontal rootstock, culms of the. season often rising from branches thickly covered with pubescent scales which are the bases of the leaf sheaths of previous seasons; new growth, rather glaucous throughout. *Culm* ascending, slender, terete, smooth, branching below, 6 to 12 inches tall. *Leaves* of sterile culms, and radical, numerous, with flat blades 1 to 2 inches long; of culm 2 or 3; sheaths usually much shorter than internodes, close, smooth; blade flat or folded, hispid on the back of the midnerve toward the rigid point, 1 line wide, 1 to 2 inches long; ligule a dense row of minute stiff bristles, ¼ line long. *Inflorescence* unisexual, flowers on distinct culms. *Male flowers* forming a short, close panicle of 5 to 8 spikelets on short pedicels, often subtended by a narrow bract on the rachis. Spikelets 15- to 30-flowered, 2 to 3 lines wide, ½ to 1¼ inches long, rachilla glabrous, internodes ⅔ line long; first and second glumes equal, narrowly lanceolate, acute, carinate, scarious, smooth, 1-nerved, 2 lines long; floral glumes lance-ovate, acute or often with short awn and 2 or 4 teeth at apex, scarious, 3-nerved, smooth, 2½ to 3½ lines long; palet oblong, flat, with margins infolded, scabrous on the two nerves.

Female flowers forming an irregular narrow panicle of 3 to 7 few-flowered spikelets, each subtended by a narrow bract; first glume narrowly lanceolate, with long, tapering point, smooth, obscurely 5-nerved, 4 to 6 lines long; second glume lanceolate, smooth, 3-nerved, 6 to 8 lines long; internodes of rachilla 1 line long, stipe bristly pubescent; floral glume linear, 4 to 5 lines long, the 3 nerves terminating in slender twisted awns, 2 to 5 inches long, with membranaceous expansions at the sides between each awn; palet lanceolate, acute or somewhat lacerate at the apex, hispid on the 2 nerves above, scarious margins folding closely over the grain, 4 to 5 lines long.

Grain light amber color, cylindrical, bifid at top, 2 lines long.

PLATE XXX; 1, staminate plant; 2, pistillate plant; *a*, staminate flower; *b*, pistillate spikelets partly dissected and the awns cut off; *c*, floral glume of pistillate flower spread out, dorsal view.

Western Texas and Arizona to Mexico.

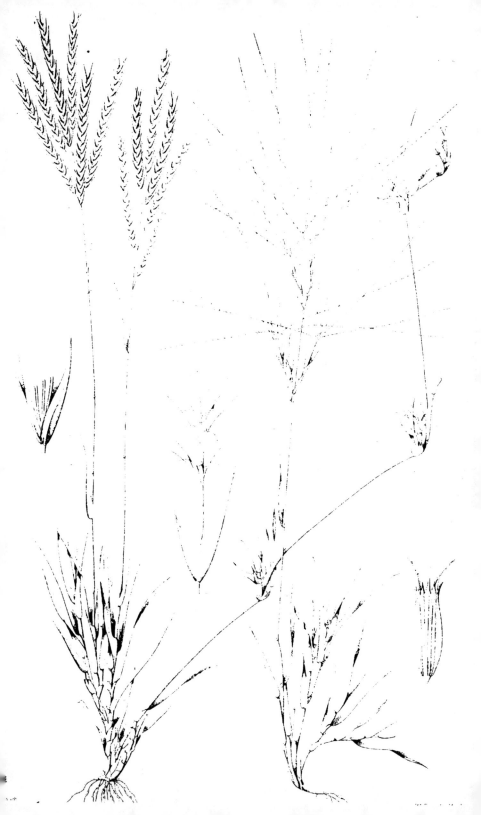

No. 31.

MUNROA SQUARROSA Torr. (*Crypsis squarrosa* Nutt.)

Plant annual, low, glaucous, more or less wooly throughout or glabrous except at the nodes.

Root slender, filiform.

Culms tufted, spreading, often prostrate, fasciculately branched, primary stems 2 to 4 inches long, secondary shorter, naked internodes striate, angular, and hispid on the angles.

Leaves ; radical and from sterile culms numerous, with flat blades ½ to 1 inch long; of stem several, crowded with the spikelets at the nodes, or ends of branches; sheaths short, membranaceous, 7-nerved, ciliate; blade flat, hispid, ciliate, acute, ¼ to 1 inch long; ligule a row of short, fine hairs.

Inflorescences hidden in the tufts of leaves at the nodes and ends of branches.

Spikelets 3- to 5-flowered, crowded in dense clusters at the apex of the branches; first glume narrowly lanceolate, hyaline, 1-nerved, 1¼ lines long; second glume same but ¼ line longer ; floral glumes herbaceous, becoming coriaceous, 3-nerved, tufts of pubescence on lateral nerves and near base of keel, entire or 2-toothed, 2 to 2½ lines long, the central nerve excurrent in a short awn ; palet narrow, hyaline, pubescent on the two nerves complicate ; upper flower in spikelets usually sterile.

Grain translucent, cream-white, lance-oval, ¼ to ¼ line long.

PLATE XXXI ; 1, cluster of spikelets; 2, spikelet; 3, second empty glume: 4, first empty glume ; 5, floral glume, side view, and 6, same spread out, dorsal view ; 7, palet ; 8, pistil ; 9, mature grain.

A low, tufted grass growing on elevated plains from Mexico to British America, usually associated with *Buchloë dactyloides*, but not liked by cattle.

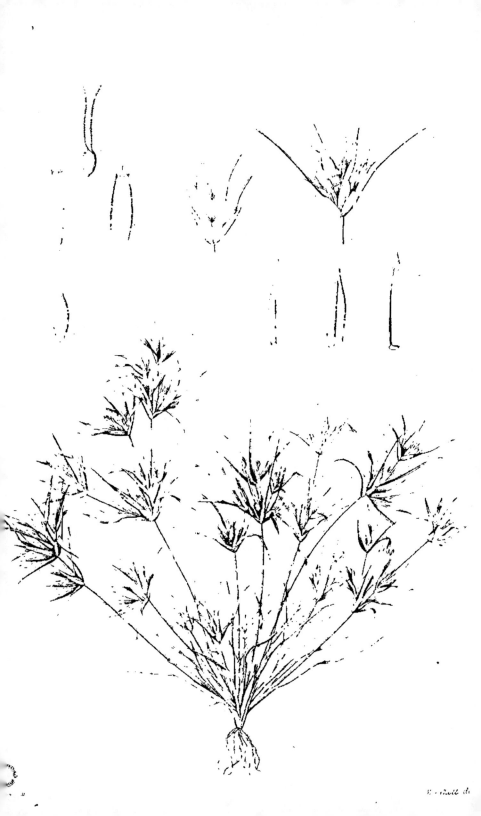

TRIODIA ACUMINATA (Munro.) Vasey. (*Tricuspis acuminata* Munro in Herb.)

Plant annual or short-lived perennial, tufted with rather bulbous base.

Culms erect, slender, not branching, slightly compressed, smooth or sparsely pubescent, 6 to 12 inches tall.

Leaves ; radical, numerous, with short, tapering, compressed sheaths, and flat or folded, abruptly pointed, pubescent blades, 2 to 3 inches long; of culms 2 or 3; sheaths mostly shorter than internodes, close, nearly smooth; blades like those of radical leaves but shorter; ligule a minute, bristle-like fringe.

Inflorescence a contracted, close head or panicle, 1 to 2 inches long, light colored or often purplish, composed of 7 to 15 nearly sessile, densely flowered spikelets or branches, ½ to ¾ inch long, sometimes interrupted below.

Spikelets lanceolate, compressed, 9-, to 12-flowered, 2 to 3 lines wide, 5 to 7 lines long; internode of pubescent rachilla less than ¼ line long; first glume ovate, acuminate, or awl-pointed, carinate, scarious, smooth, 1-nerved, 2 to 2¼ lines long; second glume same but nearly ½ line longer; floral glumes ovate, acuminate, slightly obtuse or somewhat 2-toothed at apex, carinate, membranaceous, pubescent on the 3 nerves at base, 2 to 2½ lines long, 2 lateral nerves marginal, midnerve excurrent in a short slender awn ; palet lanceolate, finely pubescent on the two prominent keels and at base, 1 to 1½ lines long.

Grain irregularly spindle shaped, light-green, ⅓ line long.

PLATE XXXII ; *a,* spikelet ; *b,* empty glumes; *c,* floral glume ; *d,* palet.

Texas to Arizona, and Mexico.

No. 33.

TRIODIA ALBESCENS (Munro.). (*Tricuspis albescens* Munro in Herb.)

Plant perennial, with slightly thickened base, smooth and often glaucous throughout.

Roots coarse.

Culms loosely tufted, erect, solid, terete, not branching, 15 to 30 inches tall.

Leaves; radical, sheaths short and open; blades flat or folded, involute, slender-pointed, 2 to 3 lines wide, 5 to 12 inches long; of culm 2 to 4, sheaths shorter than internodes, open above; blades like those of radical leaves; ligule a dense line of short, fine hairs.

Inflorescence a slender, contracted, close panicle, somewhat interrupted below, erect or slightly nodding, ½ inch wide, 4 to 8 inches long; branches appressed, unequal, ½ to 1½ inches long, bearing along their entire length rather crowded short-pedicelled spikelets.

Spikelets oval, compressed, 8- to 12-flowered, 2¼ to 3 lines long and ½ as wide; first and second glumes nearly equal, second, slightly larger, broadly ovate, acute, carinate, hyaline, smooth, 1-nerved, 1½ lines long; internodes of rachis curved, ¼ line long or less; floral glume broadly-elliptical, 3-nerved, emarginate or nearly entire, hyaline, smooth, or nearly so, midnerve slightly if at all excurrent, lateral nerves not marginal; palet broadly ovate, obtuse, 2-keeled with the margins folded flat, 1¼ lines long.

Grain elliptical, yellow, ½ line long.

PLATE XXXIII; *a*, spikelets; *b*, empty glumes; *c*, floral glumes; *d*, palet.

Texas and New Mexico.

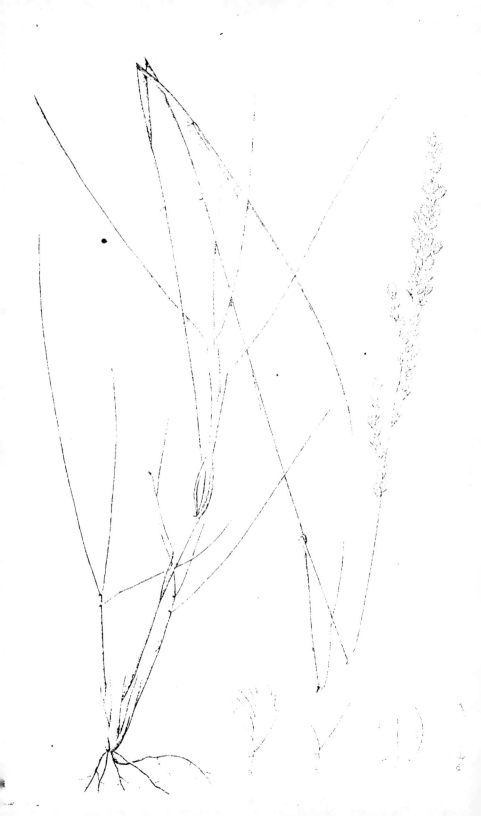

TRIODIA ERAGROSTOÍDES Vasey & Scrib.

Plant annual or short-lived perennial, with slightly thickened base.
Culms erect, branching, solid, terete, smooth, 2 to 3 feet tall.
Leaves; radical, few; of culm 5 to 9, sheaths usually exceeding the internodes, rather loose and open above, striate and slightly scabrous, blades flat or involute toward the long tapering point, scabrous on both sides. 2 to 3 lines wide, 6 to 10 inches long; ligule membranaceous, truncate, lacerate, tawny, 1 line long.

Inflorescence a loose, spreading, lance-ovate, or pyramidal, erect or drooping panicle 8 to 12 inches long; rachis angular, hispid near top, branches mostly alternate, slender, scabrous only toward the extremities, sometimes reflexed at maturity, 3 to 6 inches long, bearing the nearly solitary spikelets on slender, scabrous pedicels 1 to 3 lines long.

Spikelets oblong-ovate, compressed, 7- to 9-flowered, 2 to 3 lines long; first glume linear-lanceolate, acute or acuminate, 1-nerved, 1 line long; second glume ovate-lanceolate, acuminate and longer; internodes of slender glabrous rachilla articulating above, ¼ line long; floral glumes oblong, truncate or slightly 2-lobed, mucronate, rounded on back, membranaceous, often purplish, pubescent near the base on the 3 nerves, lateral nerves near the margins, 1 line long; palet lance-oblong, truncate, minutely ciliate, membranaceous, smooth, 2-keeled, scarcely 1 line long.

Grain oblong, angular, 2-horned at apex, opaque, brown, falling with spikelet, usually disarticulate above empty glumes.

PLATE XXXIV; *b*, spikelet enlarged.

Florida, Texas to Mexico. A large leafy grass which promises to be serviceable in agriculture.

No. 35.

TRIODIA GRANDIFLORA Vasey.

Plant perennial, with tufted bulbous base, rather glaucous or minutely cinerous-pubescent throughout.

Culms slender, erect, not branching, often geniculate at the hairy nodes, terete, sparingly pubescent, 1 to 2 feet tall.

Leaves; radical, numerous with compressed, equitant, hairy-fringed sheaths and flat or folded, white-margined, pubescent, obtuse or abruptly pointed blades, 2 to 4 inches long; of culm 3, rarely 2 or 4; sheaths half as long as internode, close, slightly pubescent or nearly glabrous; blades like those of radical leaves but upper ones shorter and erect.

Inflorescence a close, contracted, head-like white panicle, composed of numerous, nearly sessile branches, 1 to 2 inches long; rachis and branches somewhat pubescent, or scabrous.

Spikelets nearly sessile, oblanceolate, compressed, 4- to 6-flowered, 2 lines wide, 4 to 5 lines long; first glume lance-ovate, acute, carinate, membranaceous, minutely scabrous on keel, 1-nerved or sometimes 3-nerved on lower spikelets, 2 to 3 lines long; second glume same, but ciliate at base, always 1-nerved, and 1 line longer; floral glume lance-ovate, obtuse and minutely ciliate, or with 2 narrow lobes at apex, pubescent below, profusely ciliate, 3-nerved, 2 to 3 lines long; hispid mid-nerve excurrent in an awn ½ to 1 line long; palet broadly lanceolate, pubescent at the base and on the 2 prominent keels, 1 to 1½ lines long.

Grain not present in the specimens examined.

PLATE XXXV; *a* and *b*, floral glumes showing the extremes of variation at the apices; *c*, palet.

This species has been called *T. avenacea* H. B. K., from which it differs in its much larger size, and in its flowers, as is shown by a comparison of the figure in H. B. K.

Western Texas to Arizona and Mexico.

No. 36.

TRIODIA NEALLEYI Vasey.

Plant perennial, tufted, with a bulbous base.
Culms erect, slender, not branched, terete, smooth, 1 to 2 feet high, nodes ciliate.
Leaves; radical with pubescent, fringed, scarious-margined sheaths, tapering into narrow, folded, nearly smooth blades 2 to 6 inches long; of culm 3 or 4, sheaths close, smooth, lower ones equaling or exceeding internodes, upper much shorter; blades flat or folded, nearly smooth, 1 to 3 inches long; ligule a narrow, callous line with a loose fringe of hairs.
Inflorescence a dense spike-like panicle, white, 1 to 2¼ inches long, the branches ½ to 1 inch long, alternate, closely appressed.
Spikelets broadly oblanceolate, compressed, 1½ to 2½ lines wide, 2½ to 3 lines, long, 4- to 7-flowered; first glume ovate, acute, carinate, translucent, smooth, about 2 lines long; second glume same, but ½ line longer; floral glumes oblong, truncate, translucent, profusely ciliate on the margins and pubescent on the back below, 2-lobed or cleft one-third way to base, the two minutely ciliate lobes equaled or exceeded by the intermediate awn, 3-nerved, lateral nerves marginal; palet lanceolate, strongly arched, thin, pubescent on the two prominent keels.
Grain pale translucent-green, shaped like the quarter of a sphere with brownish opaque projection extending along the axis, ¾ line long.

PLATE XXXVI; *a,* spikelet; *b,* empty glumes; *c,* floral glume, dorsal and side view; *d,* palet.

Thus far collected only in Texas, by G. C. Nealley, for whom it is named.

No. 37.

TRIODIA PULCHELLA H. B. K. (*Uralepis pulchella* Kth.)

Plant a low, tufted perennial, with bulbous base, arising from a slender creeping rootstock.

Culms spreading, fasciculately branched, at the extremity of long, naked internodes.

Leaves; radical and of culm alike, numerous, clustered at the base, and around the fascicles of branches leaving the internodes naked; sheaths short, open, tapering, scarious; blades narrow, folded and involute; ligule a minute fringe, decurrent down the membranaceous margin of the sheath.

Inflorescence, small clusters of light-colored spikelets terminating the short clustered branches.

Spikelets lanceolate, compressed, 7- to 10-flowered, 2 lines wide, 3 to 4 lines long; internode of rachilla articulate below, ¼ line long; first glume lance-ovate, acuminate, carinate, hyaline, smooth, 1-nerved, 2 to 2½ lines long; second glume same but ¼ line longer; floral glume oblong, 2 lines long, cleft above half way to base or more, making 2 long narrow margined lobes, between which the midrib is extended as an awn longer than the lobes, 2 lateral nerves nearly marginal, profusely ciliate, pubescent below; palet oblong, truncate, thin, pubescent below, and on the 2 keels.

Grain pear shaped, translucent, light yellowish color, with opaque, brownish base ½ line long.

PLATE XXXVII; 1, young plant; 2, plant in flower; 3, at maturity; *a*, spikelet; *b*, empty glumes; *c*, floral glume, dorsal and side views; *d*, palet.

Texas to California and Mexico.

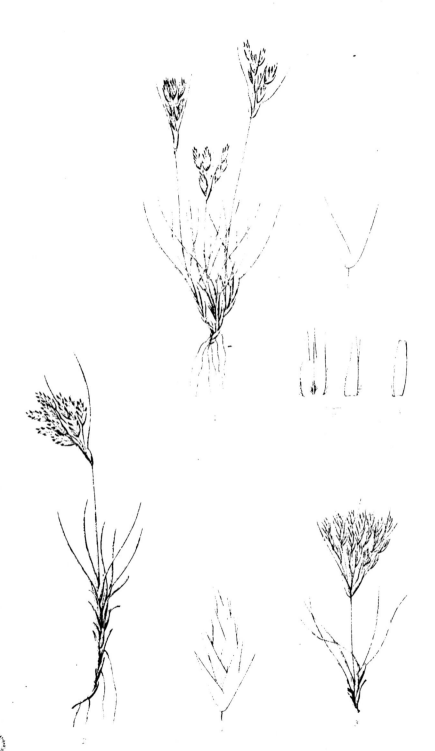

TRIODIA STRICTA (Nutt.) Vasey. (*Tricuspis stricta* Thurb. *Windsoria stricta* Nutt.)

Plant coarse, apparently perennial, glabrous throughout except near the ligule.

Culms erect, few in a place, tufted, with sterile culms at base, not branched, terete, thick, 2 to 3 feet tall.

Leaves; radical and from radical shoots numerous, the long tapering sheaths continuing with but slight constriction at the ligule, into the flat or involute smooth blade, 2 lines wide, 8 to 12 inches long; of culm 4 or 5, sheaths usually exceeding the internodes, opon above, blade like those of radical leaves, ligule an inconspicuous, tawny fringe.

Inflorescence a constricted, dense, erect, spike-like panicle, 4 to 12 inches long, branches sessile, alternate, appressed, ½ to 1 inch long.

Spikelets nearly sessile, obovate, compressed, 5- to 8-flowered, 1½ to 2 lines wide, 2 to 2½ lines long; first and second glumes equal, narrowly lanceolate, longer than the spikelet, acute, or irregularly toothed at apex, carinate, membranaceous, smooth, 1-nerved, 2 to 3 lines long; floral glumes oblong, toothed at apex, obtuse, membranaceous, 3-nerved, lateral nerves nearly marginal, middle one slightly excurrent, all pubescent below, 1 to 1½ lines long; palet elliptical, obtuse, arched, thin, the 2 keels minutely velvety pubescent.

Grain obovate, 2-horned at summit, opaque, yellow, ⅔ line long.

PLATE XXXVIII; *a*, spikelet; *b*, empty glumes; *c*, floral glume dorsal and side views; *d*, palet, dorsal and ventral views.

Louisiana to Texas and Indian Territory.

No. 39.

TRIODIA TEXANA Watson.

Plant perennial, with somewhat bulbous, tufted base.

Culms erect, simple or sparingly branched, slightly geniculate, terete, slightly pubescent, 1¼ to 2 feet tall.

Leaves; radical numerous, with short, smooth sheaths and involute blades 3 to 6 inches long; of culm 3 or 4; sheaths usually exceeding internodes, close, nearly smooth; blades flat or becoming involute, slender, pointed, smooth or slightly pubescent, 2 or 3 lines wide, 6 to 10 inches long; ligule a minute fringe with longer hairs at the sides.

Inflorescence a loose, nodding or flexuous panicle, 3 to 5 inches long; branches mostly alternate and spreading, slender, smooth, 1 to 2 inches long, divided and bearing beyond the middle 3 to 5 or more pedicellate spikelets.

Spikelets large, oblong, somewhat compressed, purplish, 6- to 9-flowered, 3 to 5 lines long; first glume ovate-lanceolate, acute or irregularly toothed, carinate, hyaline, smooth, 1-nerved, 1 to 1¼ lines long; second glume same but ¼ line longer; internode of rachilla curved, glabrous, articulate above, ¼ line long; floral glumes nearly orbicular, slightly lacerate above, membranaceous, pubescent toward the base of the 3 nerves, 2 lateral nerves not marginal, about 2 lines long; palet broad at base, narrowed above, obtuse, 2 keeled, smooth, 1¼ lines long.

PLATE XXXIX; *a*, spikelet; *b*, empty glumes; *c*, floral glume; *d*, palet, ventral view.

Louisiana to Texas, New Mexico and Mexico.

No. 40.

TRIODIA TRINERVIGLUMIS (Munro) (*Tricuspis trinerviglumis* Munro in Herb.)

Plant perennial, with slightly thickened tufted base.

Culms erect or geniculate below, rarely branching, terete, hispid, 2 to 3 feet tall.

Leaves; radical and of radical shoots numerous, with loose, pubescent sheaths and involute, hispid, often pubescent blades, 3 to 6 inches long; of culm 4 to 6; sheaths longer than internodes, open above, upper ones nearly smooth; blades like those of radical leaves; ligule an inconspicuous fringe.

Inflorescence a narrow, erect, spike-like panicle, 4 to 8 inches long; branches erect, simple, almost appressed, ½ to 2 inches long, or often reduced to single spikelets a little distant, or interrupted.

Spikelets oblong or oblanceolate, but little compressed, 7- to 9-flowered, 3 to 5 lines long; first glume lanceolate, obtuse or nearly acute, carinate, scarious, 7-nerved, 2 to 3 lines long; second glume lance-ovate, acute, carinate, scarious, scabrid, hispid on keel, 3-nerved, 2¼ to 3½ lines long; internode of rachilla stout, pubescent, articulate above, ½ line long; floral glumes oblong-ovate, obtuse, emarginate, mucronate or entire at apex, 3-nerved, pubescent below, lateral nerves vanishing before reaching the margin, palet ovate, obtuse, pubescent on the 2 keels, 1½ lines long.

Grain ovate-conical, deeply hollow on one side, dark-brown, punctate, 1¼ lines long.

PLATE XL; *a*, spikelet; *b*, and *b'*, empty glumes; *c*, floral glume dorsal and side views; *d*, and *e*, palet, ventral and side views.

Prevails throughout Texas, westward to Arizona, and northward to Colorado. Apparently not of great agricultural importance. *Tricuspis mutica* Torr. appears to be a smaller form, with shorter, interrupted panicle.

No. 41.

DIPLACHNE FASCICULARIS P. B. (*Leptochloa fascicularis* Gray.)

Plant annual, glaucous or light green, more or less purplish on the sheaths and inflorescence.

Roots numerous, coarse.

Culms few, loosely tufted at base, erect or decumbent, branching, striate, smooth, 2 to 3 feet tall.

Leaves; radical and from sterile culms with thin, smooth, striate, equitant sheaths and slender involute, slightly hispid blades, 1 line wide unrolled, 6 to 12 inches long; of stems 3 or 4; sheaths usually exceeding internodes, smooth; blade like that of radical leaves, upper one exceeding panicle and sheathing its base; ligule membranaceous, triangular, ovate, acute, entire, wider than blade, 1¼ to 2 lines long.

Inflorescence a loose, narrow, spreading panicle, included at base in upper sheath, 6 to 8 inches long; of many linear, spike-like spreading branches, hispid, mostly alternate, 2 to 4 inches long, bearing 8 to 15 nearly sessile, appressed spikelets; general rachis angular, hispid.

Spikelets linear-oblong, or lanceolate at maturity, flattened, 6- to 9-flowered, 3½ to 4 lines long; internodes of articulate rachilla, ¼ line long; first glume varying from ovate-lanceolate to linear, barely acute, or acuminate, hispid on back, 1-nerved, 1 to 1¼ lines long; second glume lanceolate to oblong, longer and often somewhat 3-toothed or lacerate at the apex; floral glumes linear-oblong, acute, ciliate on the lower third of the nerve, and pubescent at the base, 1½ to 2 lines long, 3-nerved, 2 lateral nerves marginal, ending in rather inconspicuous teeth, midnerve excurrent in a hispid awn nearly ½ line long; palet linear, with two prominent pubescent nerves, narrow, hyaline, infolded margins, and truncate or slightly rounded, minutely ciliate apex.

Grain surrounded with rather loose, hyaline pericarp; salmon pink with small garnet scar at base, flat, lanceolate, 1 line long; readily shelling out of flower as the spikelet falls.

PLATE XLI; *a,* spikelet; *b,* empty glumes; *c,* floral glume, dorsal and side view; *d,* palet.

This species presents considerable variation in the spikelets, forming probably several varieties.

It is extensively distributed over the country, both north and south, but becomes abundant in Texas and westward, also in Mexico.

DIPLACHNE IMBRICATA (Thurb.) Scrib. (*Leptochloa imbricata* Thurb.)

Plant annual or short-lived perennial from bulbous base, somewhat glaucous, purplish on the sheaths and with dark green panicle.

Culms tufted, erect, geniculate, branching, hollow, terete, smooth or minutely scabrid near base of panicle, 1 to 2 feet tall.

Leaves; radical and of radical shoots, numerous, with smooth, tapering, compressed sheaths and narrow, slender pointed, folded or involute, hispid blades, 4 to 8 inches long; of culm 3 or 4; sheaths striate, slightly roughened on upper part, open above, nearly equaling internode; blade like that of radical leaves but usually shorter; ligule membranaceous, ovate, acute, entire, wider than the blade, decurrent.

Inflorescence a rather close, narrowly-oblong panicle, 4 to 6 inches long, of numerous linear branches; rachis angular, hispid ; branches hispid, slender, mostly alternate, slightly spreading, 1½ to 2 inches long, bearing on the lower side 12 to 16 nearly sessile, appressed, and imbricate spikelets.

Spikelets linear-oblong, 7- to 10-flowered, 2½ to 3 lines long. less than 1 line wide; internodes of glabrous rachilla articulate, ⅓ line long ; first glume ovate, acute, carinate, ciliate, hispid on back, 1-nerved, ¾ line long; second glume elliptic-oblong, obtuse, often slightly mucronulate, 1 to 1¼ lines long; floral glume oblong, truncate, with two short blunt teeth at the summit, the mid-nerve terminating in a short mucro, membranaceous, pubescent on the lower half of the lateral nerves, 1 line long ; palet lance-oblong, with rounded ciliate apex, two prominent pubescent nerves and narrow infolded hyaline margin, 1 line long.

Grain light-brown, obovate, falling with flower but easily separated.

PLATE XLII; *a*, spikelet; *b*, empty glumes; *c*, floral glumes, dorsal and side view ; *d*, palet.

Texas, New Mexico, Arizona, and southern California.

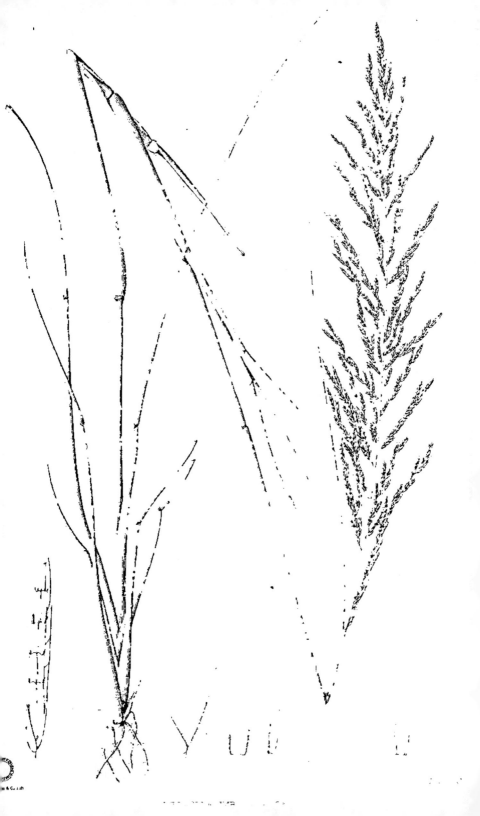

No. 43.

DIPLACHNE REVERCHONI Vasey.

Plant a low tufted annual.

Culms erect, slender, not branched, 3 to 10 inches long.

Leaves at base, numerous, involute, setose, smooth, 1 to 2½ inches long; of culms 1 or 2 above base, mostly exceeded by radical leaves; sheaths striate, close, smooth; blade filiform, involute; ligule a minute, hairy fringe.

Inflorescence a spike-like panicle, 1½ to 3 inches long; the nearly sessile, appressed spikelets alternate along the striate slender rachis.

Spikelets lance-linear, 6- to 10-flowered, 3 to 4 lines long; internode of rachilla glabrous; first glume ovate, acute, carinate, membranaceous, 1-nerved, smooth, 1 line long; second glume oblong, obtuse or obscurely toothed ¼ line longer; floral glumes 1¼ lines long, ovate-lanceolate, membranaceous, 2 teeth at apex, 2 lateral nerves slightly pubescent at base, vanishing before reaching the margin, mid-nerve excurrent into a minute hispid awn ¼ line long; palet linear-lanceolate, 2-keeled, cleft at apex, minutely ciliate, ¾ line long.

Grain light amber color, narrowly conical, falling with flower but easily separated.

PLATE XLIII; *a*, spikelet; *b*, empty glumes; *c*, floral glumes, dorsal and side views; *d*, palet.

Texas to Mexico. First collected by J. Reverchon, Texas. It has been referred to *D. simplex* Doell, from which I think it differs.

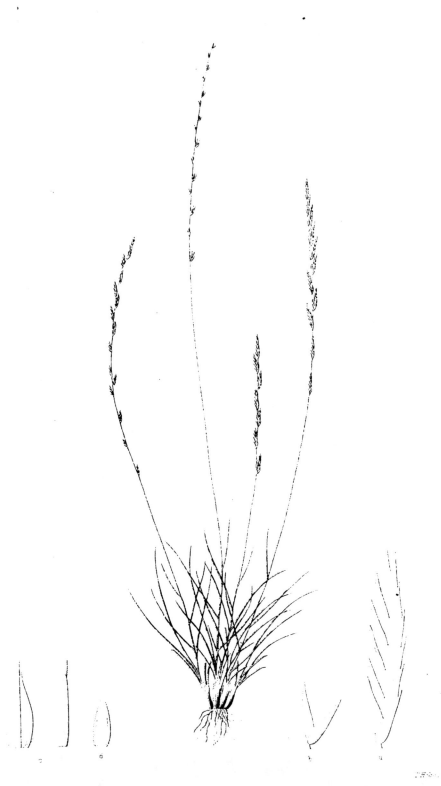

No. 44.

DIPLACHNE RIGIDA (Munro) Vasey. (*Leptochloa rigida* Munro, MSS.)

Plant perennial, from loosely tufted, bulbous base.

Culms erect, terete, smooth, not branching, 1 to 2 feet tall.

Leaves; radical and from radical shoots comparatively few, with short, loose, involute, tapering sheaths, and narrow, mostly filiform, involute, rigid, pointed blades, 2 to 6 inches long, pubescent, with few scattered hairs; of stem 2 or 3; sheaths longer than internodes, close, smooth, with blades like those of radical leaves ; ligule a prominent tuft of spreading hairs 1 line long.

Inflorescence a loose, spreading panicle 6 to 12 inches long; rachis triangular, smooth; branches distant, alternate, spreading or horizontal, triangular, hispid on the angles, with tuft of hairs at the axis, 3 to 6 inches long, bearing 5 to 8 distant, sessile, appressed spikelets.

Spikelets oblanceolate, 5- to 9-flowered, 3½ to 4½ lines long; first glume lanceolate, acute, carinate, rigid, 1-nerved. hispid on keel, 1½ lines long; second glume lanceolate, acute, convex, 5-nerved, 2 lines long; floral glumes lanceolate, acute, barely, if at all, mucronate, rigid, 2 lines long, smooth, 2 lateral nerves vanishing before reaching the margin, palet oblong, obtuse, rigid, 2-keeled, ciliate, 1¼ lines long, becoming strongly arched.

Grain oval, reddish brown.

PLATE XLIV; *a*, spikelet; *b*, empty glumes; *c*, floral glumes, dorsal and side view; *d*, palet.

Texas and New Mexico, northward to Kansas.

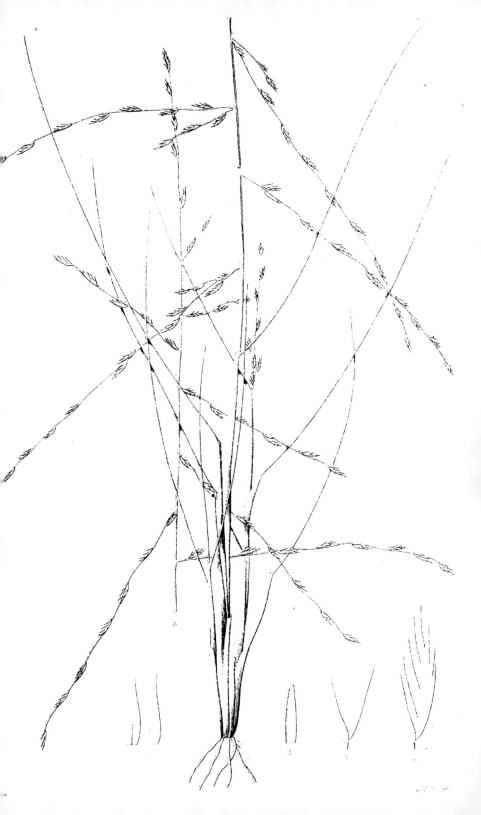

No. 45.

DIPLACHNE VISCIDA Scrib.

Plant annual or short-lived perennial, light green or somewhat purplish on sheaths and inflorescence.

Culms erect, or low and spreading from a tufted base, branching freely, geniculate, hollow, terete, smooth, 6 to 15 inches tall.

Leaves; radical and from radical shoots, few and short; of stem 3 to 5; sheaths about equaling internode, compressed, open, smooth; blade flat or folded, with slightly involute margins, somewhat scabrous above and below, 2 to 4 inches long; ligule membranaceous, truncate, lacerate, ¾ line long.

Inflorescence a rather compact, narrow, erect panicle, 2 to 3 inches long, included at the base; rachis angular, slightly hispid; branches slender, alternate, appressed or somewhat spreading at maturity, ½ to 1 inch long, bearing 6 to 10 appressed, nearly sessile spikelets on the flattened rachis.

Spikelets oblong, 4- to 6-flowered, 2 to 2½ lines long; internode of slender rachilla articulate below, ¼ line long; first glume ovate, acute, hyaline, scabrous on the single nerve, 1 line long; second glume same, scarcely ¼ line longer; floral glumes elliptical-oblong, 1 line long, 2 hyaline lobes or teeth at summit somewhat lacerate, lateral nerves nearly marginal, pubescent below, vanishing in the margin in very obscure teeth, mucronate awn of mid-nerve ½ line long; palet elliptic-oblong, hyaline, with 2 scabrous nerves and shallow cleft apex, minutely ciliate.

Grain light, opaque amber, with brown scar, elliptic, flattish, ½ line long, falling with flower or spikelet nearly complete.

PLATE XLV; *a,* spikelet; *b,* empty glumes; *c,* floral glumes, dorsal and side views; *d,* palet.

New Mexico, Arizona, and Mexico.

No. 46.

ERAGROSTIS CURTIPEDICELLATA Buckley.

Plant perennial, tufted with numerous abortive culms at bulbous base.
Roots coarse, with dense, tawny root hairs.
Culms stout, erect, rarely branching, terete, nearly solid, smooth, 1 to 2 feet tall.
Leaves of sterile culms rather numerous, with more or less involute blades 3 to 6 inches long; of stem 4 to 8; sheaths exceeding the internodes, open and rather loose above, smooth or with few scattered hairs along the exposed margins; blade involute toward the tapering point, 2 to 2½ lines wide, 4 to 6 inches long, smooth, rigid; ligule and throat, a row of fine hairs 2 to 2½ lines long; sheaths and lower sides of leaf often glandular viscid.
Inflorescence an oblong pyramidal erect panicle 8 to 12 inches long; spreading branches 3 to 5 inches long, much subdivided, mostly alternate, with tufts of white hairs in the axils, the solitary appressed spikelets borne mostly on strict, hispid lateral branchlets.
Spikelets, oblong-linear, less than 1 line wide, 2 to 3 lines long, often purplish, on hispid pedicels less than half their own length, internodes of the slightly zigzag rachilla ¼ line long; first and second glumes ovate, acute, carinate, thin, herbaceous, 1-nerved, minutely hispid on keel above, ½ line long; floral glumes lanceolate, acute, prominently nerved, ¾ line long; palet linear, curved so that its two pubescent nerves appear outside of the flowering glume.
Grain, amber color, narrowly cylindrical, ¼ line long.

PLATE XLVI; *a*, spikelet; *b*, empty glumes; *c*, floral glume; *d*, palet. The figure does not show the hairy ligule.

This species is closely related to *E. pectinacea*, being less diffuse, with shorter branches and larger spikelets.

It seems to be pretty closely confined to Texas and northward to southern Kansas.

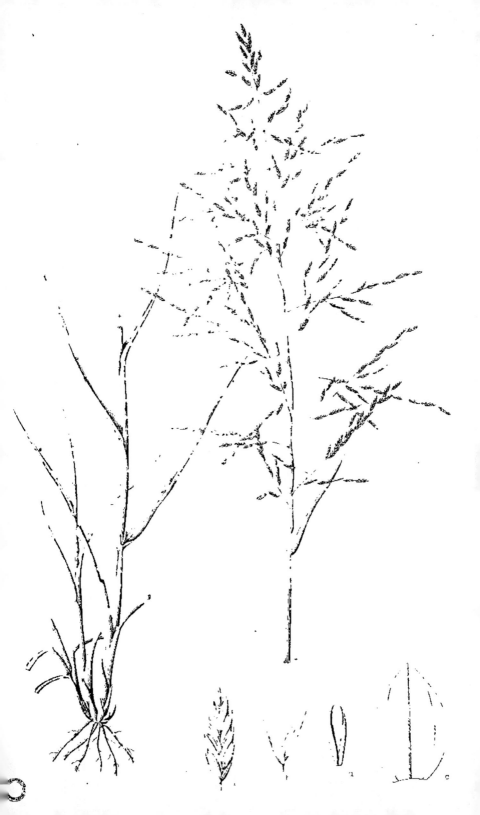

No. 47.

ERAGROSTIS LUGENS Nees. (*Eragrostis pilifera* Scheele ?)

Plant perennial, from a slightly bulbous base.

Roots numerous, rather coarse, long, not branching, and with few fibrillæ.

Culms tufted, slender, erect, simple, solid, nearly terete, smooth, 1½ to 3 feet tall.

Leaves; the lower from abortive culms, with scarious sheaths, and slender, involute blades, 3 to 6 inches long; of stem 3 or 4; sheaths ¾ length of internode, striate, loose, smooth; blade flat below, involute toward the long, tapering point; a few scattered hairs above the ligule, otherwise smooth, 3 to 6 inches long; ligule a prominent line of crowded, white hairs, 2 lines long.

Inflorescence a loose, erect, pyramidal panicle, 8 to 10 inches long, included at base in upper sheath when young, rachis grooved above each branch; branches capillary, mostly alternate, minutely scabrous toward the ends, and bearing a few white hairs at the axils, flexuous, lower ones 3 to 6 inches long, subdividing nearly to the base, bearing 15 to 20 spikelets on the long, filiform branchlets.

Spikelets linear-lanceolate, 4 to 5 lines long, on slender pedicels as long as themselves, or much longer, 5- to 11-flowered; internodes of rachilla ¼ line long; first and second glumes nearly alike, scarious margined, broadly ovate, nearly acute, obscurely 1-nerved, 1 .line long; floral glumes scarious above, broadly ovate, obscurely 3-nerved, smooth, 1 to 1¼ lines long; palet linear, membranaceous, arched, smooth, 1 line long.

Grain reddish brown, rhomboidal, ¼ line long.

PLATE XLVII; *a,* spikelet with pedicel; *b,* empty glumes; *c,* floral glume dorsal and side views; *d,* palet and stigmas. The plate does not represent the hairs of the ligule.

Texas and New Mexico.

This species is very near our *E. capillaris,* and varies considerably in the length of leaves and size of panicle; it is also near *Eragrostis Mexicana* Link.

ERAGROSTIS OXYLEPIS Torr. (*Poa interrupta* Nutt.)

Plant annual or a short-lived perennial, from slightly enlarged base, ligh green, usually tinged with purple, especially in the inflorescence.

Roots with abundant coarse root hairs, sometimes branching.

Culms ascending, prominently geniculate, hollow, not branching, teret smooth, 1 to 2 feet tall.

Leaves numerous; from abortive culms, involute, 8 to 12 inches long; of ste 2 or 3; sheaths nearly equaling or usually exceeding the lower internodes, smoot open above but appressed to culm, blade involute with slender rigid point, 3 to inches long; ligule a dense tuft of fine hairs 2 lines long.

Inflorescence an irregular, oblong panicle, of dense clusters of spikelets near. sessile on the branches, which are short above, the lower sometimes 1 to 3 inch long, erect, and at irregular intervals on the rachis.

Spikelets oblong-lanceolate, compressed, 2 to 3 lines wide, 7 to 9 lines long, 2 to 30-flowered; internodes of zigzag rachilla $\frac{1}{4}$ line long, with minute pubescence each node; first glume narrowly ovate, acute, carinate, 1-nerved, hispid on th keel, scarcely 1 line long; second glume same as first but $\frac{1}{2}$ line longer; floral glum ovate, acute, carinate, hispid on keel above, 3-nerved, $1\frac{1}{2}$ to 2 lines long; pal elliptical, cleft at apex, ciliate on the two reflexed arched marginal nerves, 1 to lines long.

Grains not abundant, translucent amber color, narrowly conical, nearly line long.

PLATE XLVIII, 1; *a*, empty glumes; *b*, floral glume dorsal and side view *c*, palet.

PLATE XLVIII, 2; another form, with panicle more interrupted and branch longer; *a'*, empty glumes; *b'*, floral glume, dorsal and side views; *c'*, palet.

Gulf States, Texas, and northward to Kansas.

ERAGROSTIS PURSHII Shrad.

Plant annual, diffuse, spreading from a tufted base.

Roots sometimes secondary from lower nodes, seldom branched.

Culms ascending, often prominently geniculate, slightly compressed, and grooved or flattened above each sheath, smooth, often branching below, 15 to 20 inches tall.

Leaves of sterile culms rather numerous, with flat or slightly involute blades 3 to 6 inches long; of stem 3 or 4; sheath 1 to 2 lines wide, 4 to 7 inches long; ligule a spreading tuft of fine white hairs 1$\frac{1}{4}$ lines long.

Inflorescence a rather loose, oblong panicle, 5 to 7 inches long; rachis angular, somewhat flexuous, branches 1, 2, or 3 in a place, 2 to 4 inches long, with few or no hairs at the axis, bearing 12 to 20 appressed spikelets on angular, twisted, hispid pedicels of varying lengths.

Spikelets linear-lanceolate, 5- to 10-flowered, 2 to 3$\frac{1}{2}$ lines long; internodes of slender rachilla $\frac{1}{2}$ line long; first glume ovate, acute, minutely hispid on back above, 1-nerved, $\frac{1}{2}$ line long; second glume same as first but nearly twice as large; floral glumes broadly ovate, acutish, convex, scarious, 3-nerved, $\frac{2}{3}$ to nearly 1 line long; palet linear-oblong, minutely pubescent on the 2 nerves, $\frac{2}{3}$ line long, arched, remaining on the rachilla after the seed falls with the floral glume.

Grain amber colored, oblong, $\frac{1}{3}$ line long.

PLATE XLIX; *a*, spikelet with pedicel; *b*, empty glumes; *b'*, and *b''*, apexes of empty glumes; *c*, floral glume, dorsal and side view; *d*, palet.

Texas to Arizona and Mexico. In the Northern States this species seems to be confused with *Eragrostis pilosa*.

No. 50.

ELYMUS SITANION Schultes. (*Sitanion elymoides* Raf. *Polyanthrix*
Hystrix Nees.)

Plant annual, or short-lived perennial, from rather bulbous base.
Culms tufted at base with many radical shoots, erect, unbranched, terete, hollow, nearly smooth, 6 to 18 inches tall.

Radical leaves mostly membranaceous scales, or leafless sheaths, those from
radical shoots numerous, striate, often pubescent, or nearly glabrous on sheaths
and blades below; blade flat or slightly involute, rigid, hispid above, 1½ lines wide,
4 to 6 inches long; leaves of culm 3, rarely 4; sheaths longer than internodes;
blades like those of radical shoots, ligule an inconspicuous, narrow, membranaceous line, often auriculate on one or both sides.

Inflorescence a rather loose spike 2 to 3 inches long; rachis articulate at base
of each flattened internode, and easily separating.

Spikelets 2 at each node of the rachis, nearly sessile, lanceolate, 5 to 6 lines
long, not including the awns, 1- to 5-flowered; upper flowers sterile; first and second glumes nearly equal, side by side in front of the spikelet, narrow, 2-nerved at
base, terminating in a divergent hispid awn 2 to 4 inches long; floral glumes ovate-lanceolate, acute, round on back, enveloping seed and palet, finely scabrous, indistinctly 5-nerved, terminating in a hispid awn 2 to 2½ inches long, the upper
imperfect glumes short-awned; palet lance-linear, obtuse, hispid on the two nerves,
margins reflexed, flat, one-half line wide, folded, 4 to 4½ lines long.

Grain dull brown, linear, wrinkled lengthwise, 2½ lines long, adherent to palet
and enveloping glume.

Extensively diffused over the arid and desert districts of the West, from the
Missouri to the Pacific, and from Dakota to Texas, presenting great diversity of
size and appearance. Sometimes the empty glumes are divided into three parts.

PLATE L; *a*, spikelet; *b*, floral glume; *c*, palet.

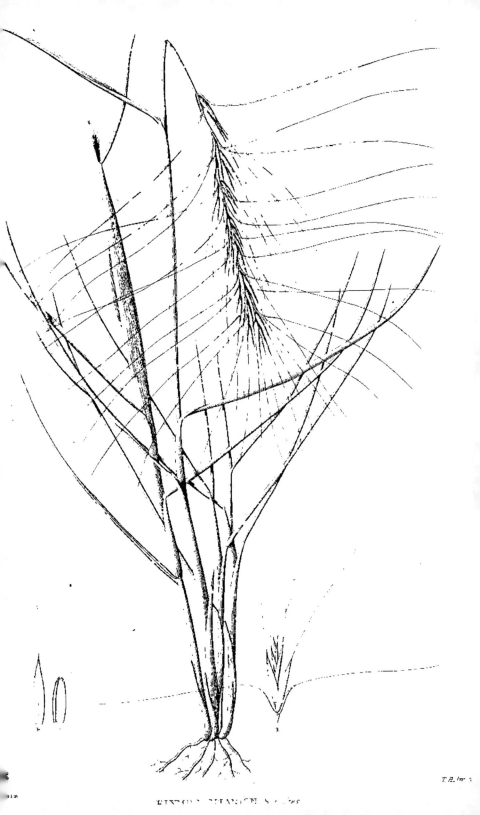

CORRECTIONS AND EMENDATIONS.

PART I.

No. 5. *Setaria caudata*, second line, Plant annual. The drawing represents a perennial form or species common in western Texas, Arizona, New Mexico, and northern Mexico. There is, however, a closely related form which is annual.

No. 11. *Hilaria mutica* Benth. It should be stated that this is *Pleuraphis mutica* Buckley. Mr. Bentham united the genus with *Hilaria*, and according to the views of some botanists Buckley's name should follow the species in parentheses; thus, *Hilaria mutica* (Buckley) Bentham.

No. 15. *Elionurus*, plate 15. The specific name at the bottom of the plate should be *barbiculmis*.

Plate 19. *Andropogon hirtiflorus* Kth. The figures *a* and *b* do not well represent the glumes of the species. It is probable that by mistake the drawings were made from spikelets of *A. scoparius*. The first empty glume should be represented as narrow and acuminate at apex, with the back scabrous-roughened and hairy.

Plate 23. *Aristida divaricata* H. B. K. This is *Aristida Humboldtiana* Trin. Trinius excludes *A. divaricata* as a mixed and uncertain species.

Plate 27. *Epicampes macroura* Kth. I was misled by the specimen in the United States Herbarium (No. 1973 C. Wright's New Mexican Coll.) in naming this species. Evidently it is not *E. macroura* Kth., which has a dense, cylindrical spicate panicle. It is *Epicampes ligulata* Scrib. Fournier in Enumeratio Mexicanarum Plantarum enumerates 13 Mexican species of *Epicampes*, of which we have too little representation to determine if our plant is among the number.

Plate 28. This is the *Cinna macroura* of Thurber in the Botany of California, but not of Kth.

Plate 29. *Chloris elegans* H. B. K. is believed to be a synonym.

Plate 32. This is *Eustachys glauca* Chap. That genus being now united to *Chloris*, it becomes *C. glauca* (Chap.) Vasey.

Plate 45. *Bouteloua stricta*. It should have been stated that this species was collected by G. C. Nealley in western Texas.

Plate 47. The figures 1 and 2 in the plate should be transposed, No. 1 being the female plant, No. 2 the male plant.

Plate 48. *Eremochloë*. This name, or one too close to it, viz, *Eremochloa* Buse, is one of earlier date for a different genus; and Professor Hackel has named our plant *Blepharidachne*.

CORRECTIONS AND EMENDATIONS.

PART II.

Plate 2. Add after the name (Thurber).

Plate 14. Transpose the numbers 1 and 2 of the plate.

Plate 30. *Karwinskiana* should be *Karwinskianus.*

Plate 33. *Albescens* should be *albescens.*

Plate 38. The name on the plate should read *Triodia stricta* (Torr.) Vasey; it was *Tricuspis stricta* Torr.

Plate 40. The name should read *Triodia trinerviglumis* (Munro). It was *Tricuspis trinerviglumis* Munro, the genus being united to *Triodia* by Mr. Bentham.

Plate 42. In like manner the name here should be *Diplachne imbricata* (Thurb.), as it was *Leptochloa imbricata* Thurb. in Bot. California.

Plate 43. Strike out the letter *s* in *Reverschoni.*

Plate 44. The name should read *Diplachne rigida* (Munro) Vasey. It was *Leptochloa rigida* Munro.

Plate 46. Add Buckl. after the name.

U. S. DEPARTMENT OF AGRICULTURE.

DIVISION OF BOTANY.

ILLUSTRATIONS OF NORTH AMERICAN GRASSES.

VOL. I.

GRASSES OF THE SOUTHWEST.

PLATES AND DESCRIPTIONS

OF THE

GRASSES OF THE DESERT REGION OF WESTERN TEXAS, NEW MEXICO, ARIZONA, AND SOUTHERN CALIFORNIA.

By DR. GEO. VASEY,

BOTANIST, DEPARTMENT OF AGRICULTURE.

PUBLISHED BY AUTHORITY OF THE SECRETARY OF AGRICULTURE.

WASHINGTON:

GOVERNMENT PRINTING OFFICE.

1891.

LETTER OF TRANSMITTAL.

WASHINGTON, *September*, 1891.

SIR: I have the honor of presenting for publication the first volume of the proposed work called "Illustrations of North American Grasses," which have been issued as Bulletin No. 12, parts I and II; and it is proposed to follow this with a second volume of plates and descriptions of the "Grasses of the Pacific Coast."

Respectfully,

GEO. VASEY,
Botanist.

Hon. J. M. RUSK,
Secretary of Agriculture.

III

GENERAL INDEX OF PLATES.

Printed in the United States
123086LV00001B/383/P

9 781409 720027